To

Lord Sheaikh

With My Compliments

I hope you will Enjoy Reading

With Kindest Regards

Jesel

14/02/2017

KING
PRAWN

Iqbal Ahmed, OBE is the Chairman and Chief Executive of Seamark plc, a company specialising in frozen seafood which was founded in 1991. Ahmed was responsible for introducing the black tiger shrimp to Europe, which transformed his family-run local shop into an internationally renowned business. As a result of this, he consistently achieved over 70 per cent export from the UK, and was one of the highest exporters from Bangladesh between the years 2002–14. He prides himself on having promoted trade between the UK and Bangladesh, and for raising the profile of the expatriate community, having experienced first-hand the challenges faced when setting up a business in a different language and culture. Ahmed holds a wide range of titles, notably Founder/first Chairman and sponsor director to the Board of NRB Bank Limited, and Chairman of UKBCCI (UK Bangladesh Catalyst of Commerce and Industry). Additionally, he was appointed an Officer of the Order of the British Empire (OBE) for services to international trade in 2001. He has used his influence to aid charitable causes in both Bangladesh and England, supporting institutions such as the Burunga Iqbal Ahmed High School and College and the Central Manchester University Hospital NHS Trust charity. A former member of the St James's Club in Manchester, he is also a member of a number of exclusive organisations in Bangladesh: the Sylhet Station Club, Chittagong Club, Gulshan Club, Bhatiary Army Golf Club, Lions Club, and Rotary Club. He lives in Wilmslow, Cheshire, with his wife, with whom he has three children.

KING PRAWN

PRAWN

DREAMING BIG AND MAKING IT HAPPEN –
THE STORY OF THE ENTREPRENEURIAL GENIUS

IQBAL AHMED

JOHN BLAKE

Published by
John Blake Publishing Limited,
3 Bramber Court, 2 Bramber Road,
London W14 9PB, England

www.johnblakebooks.com

www.facebook.com/johnblakebooks 🟥
twitter.com/jblakebooks 🟦

First published in hardback in 2017

ISBN: 978-1-78606-338-0

British Library Cataloguing-in-Publication Data:
a catalogue record for this book is available from the British Library.

Design by www.envydesign.co.uk

Printed in Great Britain by CPI Group (UK) Ltd

1 3 5 7 9 10 8 6 4 2

Text copyright © Iqbal Ahmed 2017

Papers used by John Blake Publishing are natural, recyclable
products made from wood grown in sustainable forests.
The manufacturing processes conform to the environmental
regulations of the country of origin.

Every attempt has been made to contact the relevant copyright-holders,
but some were unobtainable. We would be grateful if the appropriate
people could contact us.

TO THE THREE EXTRAORDINARY WOMEN IN MY LIFE

MY GRANDMOTHER – MY INSPIRATION

MY MOTHER – MY ROCK

MY WIFE – WHO MEANS EVERYTHING TO ME

CONTENTS

ACKNOWLEDGEMENTS

I am thankful and indebted to my late father, my mentor and role model, for his struggle to give us all a better standard of life. Without him, all of this would not have been possible.

I would especially like to thank my brothers Kamal and Bilal for being encouraging and supportive throughout my life. They have been the two pillars that have stood with me from the very beginning, in business and in life.

I have three incredibly talented children, Shahida, Manzur and Hamida: they are truly a gift. I want to thank them for understanding and appreciating my ongoing ambition to succeed in every walk of life. Words cannot describe how proud I am to say that they have grown into young successful people in their own right.

My grandchildren, Parisa and Amira: I thank them for always making me smile and keeping me young at heart.

I would like to thank my three beautiful sisters, Rahela, Shajna and Jusna for giving me such fond memories from our childhood until today.

My entire extended family have been consistently supportive and I am thankful for all the moments we have shared. I hope we continue to make more memories as our family keeps growing. I look forward to discussing the events of this book with my family at future gatherings.

I would also like to thank my valued members of staff all around the globe for their loyalty and dedication.

It is in my nature to be forthcoming and friendly with whomever I meet, whether it is through business, socially or philanthropically. Since my childhood, I have enjoyed meeting new people and developing friendships from different backgrounds and I have always been intrigued by the different walks of life that people have taken to reach the point they are at. Over time, my circle of friends has changed, some are no longer the same people I once knew and came to cherish, but I am grateful for the role they played and the lessons they taught me.

I am grateful to everyone who helped in writing this book. So much hard work has gone into it – from its inception to its publication.

I want to personally thank Stafford Hildred for approaching me in January 2013 to tell my story and for making this book possible.

Sincere thanks to my editor, Toby Buchan, for his help, guidance and expertise. I also want to thank my publisher, John Blake Publishing, for their confidence in me and for publishing my autobiography.

ACKNOWLEDGEMENTS

Lastly, my special thanks to Nita Shah for her involvement and invaluable contributions.

IQBAL AHMED, OBE

INTRODUCTION

The journey of my life has so far taken me just over 5,000 miles from Sylhet in Bangladesh to Manchester in Great Britain, sixty years that have been full of every emotion from nerve-shredding terror to great happiness. I had the great good fortune to be born into a very warm and happy family in a beautiful country village. As I grew up I realised the wonderful benefits of being a part of a solid, traditional unit with many generations of distinguished ancestors.

My childhood memories are of receiving great care and consideration from my loving parents and also having a particularly strong relationship with my grandmother. She was a very wise and kind lady who taught me many lessons about life that I still value deeply. The importance of the family values instilled in me by my grandmother was certainly the key aspect of my early education.

Life was blissful in my youngest years, but as I reached

my teens the political situation in my homeland deteriorated drastically. My father moved to England to earn money and build a new future for us. The country we now know as Bangladesh was then East Pakistan, and my early years coincided with the rise of the Bengali nationalist movement. The secure and peaceful life my family had enjoyed was ripped apart as violence grew between the Bengali people and the Pakistan army. With my own eyes I witnessed a terrible massacre of some ninety-four innocent people in the grounds of my own school and many other hideous atrocities. I will describe events in detail in the following pages, but the Liberation War (Muktijudda), or the Bangladesh War of Independence, completely transformed everything. Our comfortable existence disappeared forever and our family became, for a time, homeless refugees forced to move from relative to relative to safeguard our very existence.

I witnessed acts of heartbreaking brutality when my homeland was torn apart by the terrible conflict, but we survived. Eventually my father was able to arrange a safe passage for us all to join him. I arrived in Great Britain aged fifteen with my mother, two brothers and sister, fleeing the horrors of the war raging in our home country. My father had moved to Oldham several years earlier before the violence broke out. He had secured a job and established a home for us.

We were so relieved to be safe and together, but there were still many mountains to climb. Determined to complete my education, I spent time in London and experienced racism and rejection along the way before I was able to realise my boyhood dream of building a business. With my family all around me I have been able to create an internationally successful company that employs more than 4,000 people in many countries of the world.

Most important, I remain at the heart of a large and loving family, which is more crucial to me than all the business deals on earth. I am best known as the boss of Seamark and before I get into the details of the story of my life, I would like to set the scene, if I may, with a quick outline of the Seamark story. 'King Prawn' is not exactly my favourite nickname, but I suppose I have come to deserve it! I was the first importer of ocean tiger prawns into the United Kingdom and we still process more than a million prawns and shrimps an hour, mainly at our factory in Chittagong, Bangladesh, and through our processing plants in Manchester.

We had a small grocery shop in Oldham and lots of ambition when I joined the family business and at the end of the 1970s turned it from retail to wholesale. My brothers Kamal and Bilal joined me and created Iqbal Bros & Co. By 1984 we were importing container loads of frozen seafood. As business began to take off we moved to much bigger premises with its own cold storage in East Manchester.

As imports began to thrive it was time to generate exports from Britain. Our progress was hindered by the fact many people found it difficult, at that time, to believe that an Asian family was running a successful business. So in our push to go global we created Seamark (Seafood Marketing International Ltd) and never looked back. The next big step came in 1993 when Seamark opened its own seafood processing plant in Openshaw, Manchester. This was followed in 1997 by a much bigger operation on the seven-acre former Johnstone's paint site in Edge Lane, Droylsden.

I am delighted that the success of Seamark has allowed

me to get involved in many different kinds of charity work. I am very fortunate. I have done everything from helping to rebuild my old school to launching a bank for Non-resident Bangladeshis. As I pass my sixtieth birthday, I feel I have packed quite a lot into my first six decades. I would like to think that this book might help to show people that you can be successful and Bangladeshi. I want this to be an inspirational book. I want to show it is possible to start at the bottom and work your way up to success. I hope you will enjoy the read!

CHAPTER ONE

CHILDHOOD

I was born in the beautiful village of Siraj Nagar in the district of Sylhet in the north-east of what is now the proud country of Bangladesh, on 4 August 1956. There was not exactly a silver spoon in my mouth, but my family was prominent locally as long-established landowners and my circumstances were regarded as fortunate. Our home was a large farmhouse by a river, which was surrounded by a beautiful landscape of our own estates of small farms. The only way you could travel any distance was by boat or horse. The village was a wonderful place to be brought up in. As in any old town or city, people who build by the river build the best houses. It was like being next to the main road by today's standards, because the river was the main means of transport. Our caretakers and housekeepers live there now, but no members of our family live there, not for the last fifty years.

We do still visit when we are in Bangladesh. We have a

home in the capital city, Dhaka, and in Chittagong, and also in the main town of Sylhet. When we go there, we spend all day relaxing and on occasion stay overnight. We enjoy barbecues under the mango trees and various tropical plants that grow there. You can see miles of green countryside that is still largely unspoiled.

When I was born we owned lots of land and most of it was let out to our many tenants. Although it was only sixty years ago, when I look back to my early childhood it seems like time and knowledge has progressed enormously. Everyone back then lived without the technology we take for granted today and we had a peaceful life in a happy village set in enchanting countryside. My earliest memories are of being a much-loved oldest son of a large, warm and close-knit family. I always felt very safe and secure as I somehow knew I was very fortunate to have such warm and loving parents. As the homemaker, my mother always looked after me and my siblings so well. We were very, very close. I treated my parents with the utmost respect and never knowingly upset them with even the most trivial things.

We had many tenants who worked on our lands and lived in the houses we owned on the hundreds of nearby acres. So much has changed in my lifetime I can hardly believe the slow and gentle country life I enjoyed as a boy. It was a very relaxed lifestyle for all of us; my father was able to concentrate on enjoying life and family. Thanks to the family's position as large local landowners my father followed in the footsteps of my grandfather and had great responsibilities. He was the arbitrator for any differences between businesses, families or individuals within the village and had to be on hand to advise on many different kinds of disputes, so he was a very important person in the village. Ours was by no means an ordinary family and I would like to explain here a little about how it came to be in a position of such power and influence.

Our family had held this important position in the area for hundreds of years. The history of my family is very much a part of me even today when I live thousands of miles away in Britain; it is something that has helped to lead, drive and direct me onwards in life. Our history can be traced back to the early sixteenth century when the area was part of India under Mughal rule. The land then known as Subah Bangala, which today forms Bangladesh, was governed by Munim Khan, also known as Khan-I-Khanan.

During this time, a knowledgeable young man blessed with great vision and a tremendous personality embraced Islam. He came from a village called Taraf in Sylhet. His father was a Hindu of high caste who owned vast estates and held a high reputation in the society of the day. He tried hard to persuade his father to join him in embracing Islam, but his father refused to leave Hinduism. This is when he left his ancestral home and migrated to the village where I was born, Shiraj Nagar, with his new Muslim name of Taj Mohammad.

He had acquired a large piece of land within the village and proceeded to build the large farmhouse, which was to become my first home hundreds of years later. Taj Mohammad chose the site of the house well. He ordered building to take place for the large farmhouse that was to be our family's home for centuries, on the bank of the river known locally as the Buri Nadi (in English, River Buri). It is a tributary of the greater Buri Barak that flows down from the Indian state of Meghalaya, which is adjacent to Sylhet.

The Buri Barak is connected to the Surma and Kushiara rivers as well as the large wetland ecosystems known in

Bengali as *haors*; a large and ancient system of canals joins the Muktarpur, Kawadighi and Hakalui haors. The Buri River was the lifeline of the whole area's economy, which included trade, commerce and transport of agricultural products.

The farmhouse that Taj Mohammad built on the bank of the Buri River was set in around eighty acres of fertile land. There were large canals on the east, west, north and south sides, and large lakes on either side: the western lake was used mainly by women and children, the eastern for farming fish. The rivers and waterways were an all-important means of travel and communication for the local people in those days before roads and railways. Taj Mohammad's choice of location was crucial to the continuing prosperity of my family. We still appreciate its benefits today.

Taj Mohammad became firmly established in the area, married and had children. His son, Faazil Mohammad, was the outstanding achiever of the offspring, showing signs of great brilliance from a very young age. Taj took great care of Faazil, especially of his education, and Faazil soon became very well versed in the language of Farsi, which was the official language of the Mughal Empire. Faazil was very ambitious and keen to do the very best for the family. He saw that acquiring all the full and correct legal rights to the land and property we occupied was essential to our family's future status in society. He was an educated man with experience in the management of '*taluk*', which means the permanent lease of the land and property, so he realised that he needed the official documents to prove the family rights to land.

This meant approaching the Mughal headquarters in Delhi, which was a very complex procedure only high-profile and powerful members of society with very high morals could take on. Fortunately for our family, Faazil Mohammad had the qualities that made him capable of accomplishing this difficult, yet vital, task. In the Sarkar district of Sylhet there were eight areas of land known as *taluks* or *tehsils*, one of which was named after my famous ancestor: it is known as number 22, Taluk/Tehsil Faazil Mohammad. The Taj Mohammad dynasty was propelled vigorously on by Faazil and continued to grow further in both acquisition of land and social stature. The new properties included bodies of water, cultivatable land and fellow land for cattle grazing in the large Muktapur Haor, which was about two kilometres from the original farmhouse. Around the same time, land and farmhouses were given to a number of families in nearby villages, and these tenants, or *prozas* as they are called, offered their labour and services. The members of our family dynasty were known as *mirashdars*, which means 'landlords'.

I have a full history of my family but will only mention here one or two of the prominent persons of each generation. Danesh Mohammad, son of Faazil Mohammad, came to prominence amongst his brothers and led the dynasty. Likewise, Ishaque Mohammad, son of Danesh Mohammad, came to the forefront. A well-educated and courageous man, he was well versed in Bengali and Farsi. Besides being a renowned *olirashdar* (landowner), he was a writer of deeds, who could write fluently with both hands and even using his feet! He was a brave horse rider and owned several horses, which in those day were used mainly for travel.

Ishaque Mohammad had a cousin by the name of Jahir Mohammad. He was well educated with excellent knowledge of the Bengali language and literature. He obtained a minor school certificate and became a reputed poet and songwriter.

He has written many compositions about the Hijri month Muharram, Hazrat Imam Hasan (RA) and Imam Hussain (RA). His compositions are recited even today by the local people, especially during Ashura (10th day of Muharram), a tragic day for Muslims.

In this connection, the cousin of my grandfather Mohammad Idris Ali, Mohammad Aksir, should also be mentioned. He was the son of Zahir Mohammad and the nephew of Jahir Mohammad. Mohammad Aksir was well versed in English, Malayan and Chinese languages. He managed to establish a trading business in Singapore in the years after the First World War. Singapore was a part of Malaysia at the time. Mohammad Aksir went on to open a large bookshop in Singapore during the 1930s. When the Second World War broke out he had to go into hiding after Singapore fell to the Axis forces as he was a strong supporter of the Allies. When the Allies regained control of Singapore he came out of hiding and was able to expand his business further.

The aforementioned Ishaque Mohammad had two marriages. From the first marriage came three sons: Muhammad Yakub Ali, Muhammad Ali Kona Miah and Muhammad Idris Ali, and one sister who was married to Moulana Qazi Mobarak Ali, the Head Imam of the local mosque, and whose home was adjacent to the mosque and Moktob (Burunga Islamic School). He was well versed in Bengali, Farsi and Arabic. The status of the family in society was very high and they had four sons.

Their eldest son was Kazi Safar Ali, an Ayurvedic physician who gave medical treatments to local people. The second son, Shaukat Ali, also well versed in Farsi, Bengali and English. He was a great poet and also became the headmaster of the

Government primary school. Although he did not practise, he had a vast knowledge of the field of homeopathic medicine. He composed a book of poetry in which he describes the uses of homeopathic medicine, but this valuable book was unfortunately lost after his death. The third son, Mahmood Ali, was a recognised homeopathic physician who practised in Balaganj Upazila until his death. The fourth, Tohur Ali, is still living in England.

From Ishaque Mohammad's first marriage, his son, Muhammad Idris Ali, married Syeda Afrozunessa and they had two children: a son, the late Abdul Khalis, and a daughter, Noor Jahan. Abdul Khalis (who was to become my father) travelled to Manchester in the United Kingdom in the mid-1960s and became a self-employed businessman. He became the first Non-Resident Bangladeshi (NRB) of this dynasty. He hails from a traditional and educated family of the same village as Taj Mohammad, Shiraj Nagar in Bangladesh. Noor Jahan is also an NRB currently residing in Manchester and is married to Shafiqul Bari. He hails from a traditional and educated family also from Shiraj Nagar where he was a teacher. They had two daughters, Shelly and Yarun, and one son, Shahnur Miah.

Al Hajj Abdul Khalis married Suretun Nessa Khanom and they had six children, including myself: Iqbal Ahmed, Kamal Ahmed, Bilal Ahmed, Rahela Mohid, Saira Chowdhury and Jusna Rahman. Al Hajj Abdul Khalis passed away on 28 January 2005 and his wife Suretun Nessa Khanom on 5 August 2012. Both of those days were very sad for me.

As I said earlier, I was born in 1956 and my family history is very important to me. I might be British today, but Bangladesh is still in my heart. Business means that I travel a great deal

11

and spend time in both countries. Several times a year I love to revisit the beautiful house in which I was born – where some of the great characters I have outlined above also lived – which is still in our family's ownership and which holds so much significance for me. It is a magnificent timber house with large halls at the front and the back, which is today set on some sixteen to twenty acres.

My grandmother taught me so many things; good manners, how to be respectable and how to take care of your guests. I learned that in any generation there were always two, three or four brothers and one of them became the most prominent one and then usually led the way and handed over to the next generation. My great-grandfather used to run panchayat, a kind of law and arbitration court. He was the village leader and he was very widely respected. But when it came to my father's time things had become quite difficult economically because over the generations the land had been divided many times and many had taken their share. It slowly but surely reduced the area of the land we owned, and of course the level of income we earned from the rent.

Sylhet is a very prominent area of Bangladesh. I don't say that just because it is where I come from! In fact most of the Bangladeshi people who live in Britain come from Sylhet. It has always been one of the richest areas. When I was growing up there were no homeless or starving in the district and the people were very educated. Many people were able to live well off the lands, and a lot of the population migrated to the area from other districts in the country.

The British and their Empire arrived in the Indian province of Bengal in 1874 and started planting the tea that became such an important part of our economy. From Sylhet you can travel anywhere as the British built more than 10,000 miles of driveable roads and train lines that linked the entire subcontinent. It was done for their own work and pleasure, as they used to it travel to all the different gardens and plantations.

British control lasted until after the Second World War. When the British left and during the Partition of 1947 India was divided into two independent nations, some of people who used to live in our lands took over. It is a process that we call *javindar*. We found that some of the land in our possession was lost along with any income from rents. Tenants in some cases took the ownership of the land that was recorded in their names under Partition.

After the Second World War, in my father's time in control, there was a huge change in lifestyle. Before I was born, from what I heard from grandmother, our family was very comfortable and lived like aristocrats in their own territories. Now cash became more important; in the old days living in the countryside, you didn't need much cash. After the war, many landlords moved into the cities and towns when their rental incomes began to dry up. In the countryside huge changes took place as the population grew and farms and other works became more organised.

All the developments in technology finally started to reach our country and people's lives began to change and develop. Until thirty years ago, people in Bangladesh never worried about going to the city. They never had deep freezers or television sets. They did not spend hours on their laptops or mobile phones because these things did not yet exist. In my lifetime, modernisation has completely altered everyone's life, particularly in Bangladesh.

The arrival of technology started when my father was

young. He was the only son and he was quite an energetic, ambitious and self-driven man. He loved the arts, such as music and pottery. He used to enjoy travelling. When he was young, everything was available, but times were changing.

I remember when I was quite young I was very conscious of my position as the oldest son. I had two younger brothers, Kamal and Bilal, and my sister Rahela. So there were four of us close in age. It became apparent to me that cash was becoming more important. The money from the land rent was reduced because after Partition people who had been our tenants for generations were no longer legally obliged to pay their rent after a change in the law. They were given the land to live free. There was definitely a financial crisis in the family. My father knew he would have to think of an alternative way to earn money. This was a colossal change in our circumstances. We had never worked for anyone, and held a position in local society that came with a very privileged lifestyle.

At this time, though, I was blissfully unaware of this reduction in our income as I was still a little boy. My parents always did everything possible to make sure we enjoyed our early years to the maximum. It was a very innocent childhood and the adult I became closest too when I was young was my grandmother, Syeda Afrozun Nessa. She was a very wise woman. My grandfather, Muhammad Idris Ali, was a businessman and was working with his cousin in Singapore. He was also in the merchant navy for a time. He got married quite late in life at thirty-nine years old to my grandmother when she was only fifteen. My grandfather was extremely hard-working and was always very busy. He travelled widely all over the world because of his work.

When my great-grandfather Ishaque Mohammad used to

prepare all the deeds and legal letters, my grandmother used to write them and file them. This is how I think she gained a lot of insight into our ancestors, from the old deeds (*buri dalil*). I learned a lot about our ancestors from my grandmother. She believed it was very important to know as much as possible about your family's past. She was very bright and knew all about the local boards and the union council. She studied the British rules and laws and became very knowledgeable.

When I was growing up, I often used to help my mother and grandmother any way I could. I would do shopping for my mother when I was a little older. Starting the day was not always my strong point. I remember I often had a hard time getting going in the morning. This produced some stern reactions. If I stayed in bed too long my grandmother would simply kick me out! She would come and take the blankets off me and scream at me to get up and study! According to her you just had to wake up early in the morning and work. My grandmother thought early-morning study was better than evening study. I would drink a glass of milk from our own cattle, and she would make me study at five o'clock in the morning! Today I am grateful because I think it had a good effect on me. Now I believe in hard work. My grandmother taught me: 'Get up early, you have jobs to do!' That's the culture I was brought up with. You have to pray and you have to study. After I had studied, I would go and jump into the lake, have a swim in the fresh water and get straight out and have something to eat then go for a run! I still have a lot of energy today and I think it comes from the way I was brought up.

If my grandmother travelled to the city I used to love to go with her. She shared every bit of her knowledge with me.

She was a kind of arbitrator in the village where she was very important due to her legal background. I enjoyed my childhood very much; it was a lovely rural society. The large town of Sylhet was 19 kilometres away, but there were also small towns where you could go and do your shopping. It wasn't too far to go for a few hours and there never seemed to be any trouble or danger in our lives.

Of course I would not like to suggest that everything was perfect and everyone was good. There were naughty people. We heard stories of boys sneaking out at night and running away with the girls. That was not for me. We were not allowed out at night. In any case, it is always difficult when everyone knows you and your family. Everyone knows everything. If anyone did something wrong everyone knew. We were way behind children growing up in Britain, I would say. The first TV programme I saw was in 1969. That was in Sylhet when the father of the nation, Sheikh Mujibur Rahman, was delivering a speech. I remember I watched it in the house of one of my best friends. His father was a doctor and they had one of the first TV sets in our area. For a long time there was no television in the village; come to think of it there was no electricity or gas and we just had lanterns and kerosene lamps! But we did have the cinema in Sylhet town when I was a young boy. I used to love the Bengali films.

Our family in particular was very adventurous. We travelled all over, to Sylhet, to Dhaka, even to Singapore sometimes. It was not a big deal because you could take a train to just about anywhere in the subcontinent. The British-built railways operated very efficiently. I was young then, but there did not seem to be so much strife and violence in the world. Religious leaders were completely different. I do not believe religion was political in the old days: religion was a completely separate issue from politics and politicians were then highly respected. Most of them had fought for the country and were very distinguished and widely admired.

When I search back in my mind for my very earliest memory, I recall the day my grandmother took me to primary school. She left me there as usual and on the way back she went to my auntie's house, but when she arrived home she was surprised to see I was already there before her! She was shocked and said, 'Hey, what are you doing. I left you at school. You must stay there!' I said I didn't like it so had run home. I was in trouble with the family, but in fact it happened many times! I was caned every time I ran away! One day my grandmother screamed at the teacher, who was also from our village, 'Make sure my grandson stays at school. Why did you let him go?' My grandmother used to charge the teacher with making sure I studied well and to always look after me at school. In class I never liked to sit on the front row, I took the second or third bench and kept my head down.

Sometimes the teacher came to visit our house and I used to be very frightened whenever this happened. I used to run into the bushes in case he said something about what I had been getting up to at school. I must confess the truth: I was a naughty boy, I got up to all sorts of things. Whenever we got up to mischief, I had to lead with everything. But I used to be frightened if we got caught! Also, I had a lot of respect for my elders and if they shouted at me I used to get really scared.

We had a gang and of course I was the leader. However, much of my worst behaviour ended after I left junior school. When I passed into my high school the headmaster was my distant uncle! Mr Mashuk Ali. So, as you can imagine, I couldn't get up to any hanky-panky there. He was from our village but now lives in the USA with his family. I am still in contact with him.

I had to grow up and become much more straightforward. It was a scary moment whenever my uncle called me to his office. He was much stricter with me than he was with other boys. But I would not be put down. Sometimes I used to take a few boys out and say, 'Look we are not going to school today, we are just going out to a funfair or to a football match.' I don't know how I managed to get away with it!

CHAPTER TWO

FATHER LEAVES

I was blissfully unaware of it at the time, but the financial crisis was really hurting our family. This was a very difficult time for my father. My grandmother later explained how shocking and troubling the situation became for him. It wasn't easy for him to suddenly start a career in the civil service or the army. So with our income much reduced, my father decided to travel abroad to make the money we needed to survive. The family had a business in Singapore. In fact, we still have a business in Singapore!

My grandfather spent most of his life in Singapore. He had a lot of colourful stories to tell about that part of the world because his brother was in the British merchant navy. There were a lot of stories about Great Britain and the importance of Britishness. We admired the British a great deal, so my father and two of his friends decided to come to England to earn money. The three of them flew from our country to England at the end of 1965.

It was a very difficult time. The family was very concerned. At first we didn't really know what was happening. It was not clear exactly where my father had gone. My grandmother became worried when he didn't turn up for a while. She thought he must have taken a holiday! In those days communication was completely different. There was no telephone. If you wrote a letter it took fifteen days to go from one district to another. I was nine years old, still a little boy, so of course I was much too young to understand what was going on. My father's departure was quite dramatic and caused a great deal of consternation for all of us. Would we fly to England and join him? Would he return home soon? We didn't know and my mother and my grandmother were, understandably, concerned. For a long time we used to wait anxiously for the post to arrive to find out what was happening. I remember those airmail letters. Everybody anxious to find out exactly what had happened to my father. Eventually, it all settled down as news came back and then there was a time every week when we used to write a letter to send.

My father travelled first to London. He had a cousin who lived in Sheffield, and so he went to stay there. He was offered a job in a steel mill but after a short time, travelled on to Oldham where he lived until we arrived. He worked in a textile mill, where he became a supervisor within two years. He was quite a dominating, leader-type man, a strong person with a powerful personality.

When my father left us and travelled to England I became the man of the house, even though I was very young. I had no uncles; I was left with my mother and my grandmother. My grandfather was a very simple man and he was also quite old at that time. I was the oldest son on both my father and mother's side, so all my cousins and brothers and sisters looked up to me. Even from an early age I had the pride and the privilege. From a very young age I think I recognised that I was going to have responsibility in my life. But my family looked after me well; they were very loving and I happily accepted that everybody looked to me to be the next leader.

As I said earlier, my inspiration was my grandmother. She was a very dynamic woman who was always a great help to me. She became much more than just my grandmother: she was my best friend. When I was growing up I spent very little time with my father and a great deal of time with my grandmother. I learned a lot from her, she helped me to become what I am. She taught me how to communicate with people, how to build trust in relationships, how to behave honourably at all times and to become an honest and dignified man.

My mother, too, was a great teacher. She was kind and thoughtful and she brought us all up very well. My mother and my grandmother were both very strong-minded women so they didn't always live easily together. We had no real problems. My grandmother was in control of everything important, like finance. My mother was in control of running the house. That was very satisfactory. My father was very kind and very easy-going. He helped many people and did many kind things without the family knowing.

My childhood was great. I used to go to school almost every day, unlike lots of children in those more relaxed days. It meant walking half a mile, but that was nothing. We walked everywhere. I was quite naughty and a little cheeky as a young boy. I wasn't keen on studying or the whole process of learning, but somehow still managed to be brilliant at school! I was very good at reading. I found it easy. Perhaps I found it too easy! I never thought I would be fully educated with a university degree or some other top qualification. But from boyhood I always had it in my head that I would be a successful man. When I was at school I can remember telling my friends that my ambition was to be a businessman and be very successful. Confidence was never something I lacked. I was always determined to achieve my ambitions and confident I would achieve my aims somehow. Nowadays, you can see everything on your mobile phone or your computer, but in the old days we used to read books and magazines. I didn't really have comic-book heroes, though. My father and my uncle were my heroes! And I had other heroes, but they were always business heroes!

As far back as my earliest recollections, I always believed myself to be a unique person. I knew that, once grown up, I would want to have the very finest things: the best car; a detached house with lovely gardens; a beautiful wife and fine children. Whatever I needed, whatever luxury for my life, I would have. As a boy I knew the only way to achieve this was to have my own business, realising from an early age that if I worked for somebody else they would take most of the money and I would not get this top-class lifestyle. Nobody told me this. Somehow, at a young age, I worked it out for myself.

So when I was a little boy I knew I would work for myself, that I would create a business. I did have ideas beyond my years. I always liked to look smart too. I used to put gel in my hair and always tried to comb my hair to look tidy and smooth, but on one particular occasion the teacher said to me, 'Did you put your head in your grandmother's tin of oil or something?' My hair was so full of grease I couldn't comb it! I always felt school and lessons were much too boring and a waste of time and I would escape whenever I could. I just used to go off into the countryside or into town, and then come home just when school was finishing as if I had been there all day.

I had a lot of confidence as a boy. In normal circumstances, I was never frightened, which is a great advantage in life I've since found. My grandmother taught me I was as good as the next man and probably better. She also taught me how to build up trust with other people. There are many incidents in my childhood involving my grandmother that still have great significance for me today. For example, she used to give me pocket money to buy biscuits and things like that to eat at lunchtime. One day she was busy talking to some people and I kept whispering, 'I am running late. Please give me my pocket money.' She was very busy dealing with something and simply said, 'Get credit from somebody. Ask the shopkeeper to lend you the money.'

It sounds a simple thing, but it was one of the most frightening challenges I had encountered up until then in my young life. Yet I was determined to take it on. At lunchtime I went to this shop, grabbed some sweets, and said, 'I'll pay you tomorrow!' Then before the shopkeeper had time to think, let alone answer me, I ran away as fast as I could. My heart was beating so fast. I ran all the way home and told my grandmother what I had done. She was very surprised and said, 'Why did you do that?' I explained that I was so frightened that, although I did what she had said, I did not ask properly. She said, 'That was not a good thing. Well tomorrow, the first thing you must do is to pay back the money.'

I knew she was correct, though I felt very embarrassed by what I had done. But in the end it was all right. Although it was difficult to face the shopkeeper, I went and paid him. He said to me, 'What is your name and your father's name?' in a very serious manner. I was again frightened. I told my grandmother and she said, 'Good. You have a difficult relationship but you have built trust. Unless you ask for credit, borrow money and pay it back on time, you don't build up trust. Once you start dealing with people you need trust.'

I was eleven years old when she taught me this vital lesson, but it has stayed with me all my life. You can pay cash every day to someone, but that way you don't build up trust. She taught me that you must recognise the person you're dealing with and build up a relationship. You must learn to judge between good people and bad people. That judgment must be right – be very careful who you make friends with. A good person will never let you down whatever you do. A bad person, whatever you do, will always let you down. These are the important things I learned from her. A good person will always help you but you have to be a good person, too. Always look after them and they won't let you down.

We were quite an important family in our part of the world and there was a responsibility on me to keep our position and reputation going as previous generations had done before. We were all brought up well. You expected a lot from life and you had a lot in your life, but there was an expectation that we would behave properly and never let the family down. Most of all, I remember we were a very happy family. There was always laughter in our house. We were not especially rich, but we were much better off than some of our neighbours and whatever we had we were content with.

One incident from my youth sticks firmly in my mind. I had a fight with the son of our neighbour. I felt that he started it, because he abused me, so I thumped him. Afterwards I ran away. Later my grandfather came to me and said: 'You shouldn't have done that!' I was so sad. I said: 'I wish my father was here.' But it was the son of my father's best friend's that I had hit. I tried to explain what had happened but my grandfather took the other boy's side.

I went to my grandmother and said that this wasn't right. She took me to face the other boy the next day and explain what had happened. I said that he had abused me first, so I had no choice. My grandmother said, 'Right, well done.' I explained it was not my fault because he had said something bad about me. He swore at me so I hit him. My grandmother said I was right to stand up to him and not run away like a coward.

I think we grew up very slowly in the country in those far off days. For instance, I never had any girlfriends as a young teenager in Bangladesh. It was not allowed, and I always behaved myself. Well, almost always!

Even in my childhood, I always wanted to lead. I was always captain of the football team. My father had been a good player, so I must have got some of my ability from him. As far back as I can remember, I was happy to lead the team. I have always been a leader in team games and in the classroom. In any sort of competition I was always chosen to be so. I even wanted a leading role in any school play. I have always been choosy and confident. I don't like to follow someone else. This has been the case all my life.

CHAPTER THREE

WAR
BREAKS OUT

The lives of all the members of our family along with millions of other Bangladeshis were changed forever when the Liberation War between East and West Pakistan broke out in 1971. It was a terrible conflict that seemed to come from the language dispute that had been rumbling along since before I was born. West Pakistan wanted to impose Urdu as the official language on East Pakistan (the land which was to become Bangladesh). The East Pakistan university students protested that we had thousands of years of culture to support our use of our Bengali language. From that movement grew a belief by many in Bangladesh that we must become independent from Pakistan; violence increased and there were many incidents, which led eventually to the Bangladesh Liberation War.

The Partition of British India in 1947 had created the Dominion of Pakistan, which comprised two geographically and culturally separate areas with Indian territory between them. The western zone was called West Pakistan while the eastern zone was initially called East Bengal, and then later East Pakistan. Although the two zones had roughly equal populations all of the political power was concentrated in West Pakistan. It was widely considered that East Pakistan, where we lived, was being exploited economically. There were many long-running grievances, most of which, as a happy, sport-loving schoolboy, I was blissfully unaware.

In my earliest teenage years I began to be aware of the political struggles that were going on in our country. I was much too young to understand what was happening, of course. I realise now that in the months and years before the war actually started there was tremendous political unrest. Even in country areas, where we felt as though we lived in our own safe little world, we began to fear trouble ahead. My mother and grandmother tried hard not to worry me, but I picked up on their anxiety.

They were already feeling vulnerable with my father away in England. They tried to include me in adult conversations and I tried hard to understand what was going on, but it was never easy. The impact of the political turmoil was even felt at school. The education system seemed paralysed by the endless wrangling, so we barely attended school. In fact, after a time we could hardly go out anywhere. Everybody was filled with anxiety; there was fear everywhere. The normal activities of life more or less came to a halt, and a great many people started moving out.

Looking back with the benefit of hindsight, it seems that for at least three or four years before the Liberation War started, everybody feared something terrible was going to happen. Military rules regarding travel and other areas were introduced and they were very restrictive. Tension between nationalities and religions was rising and the atmosphere was bad everywhere. No one knew what was going to happen but it became increasingly clear that a lot of problems were looming for what were a peaceful people.

There are echoes of the situation in the world today. People who have lived happily alongside each other for many years are suddenly at daggers drawn simply because of their different religious beliefs. In our country, the Muslims, the Hindus, the Buddhists and the Christians had lived alongside each other for hundreds of years with no major problems. I could not understand why there should be any trouble in our land. At the end of the day the Bengalis, who live in what is today Bangladesh, were all Bengalis. They could have been any one of several religions – Muslim, Buddhism, Christian, Hindu – but their nationality was the same and they all spoke one language, and ate same sort of leaves. They had different beliefs and everybody respected the others'.

But the Pakistani people could not understand our culture, particularly the ruler of East Pakistan. This is where I think there was a problem. They were against the Hindus, and thought the Hindus, with the help of India, were the people creating all the problems. But I believe that was absolutely wrong. The Hindus were good people who were trying in any case to move out of the country to India, away from Pakistani control. No one blamed them, and even many of the Muslim people began to feel that this country would be roughly ruled.

That's one thing, but the worst thing was the unbalanced state of the education system. The schools were not fairly administered. We went very swiftly from being an efficient, well-ordered school to an unruly school that was unfairly administered. Before the Liberation War even began, we were forced by the student leaders to go on to the street and shout slogans against the ruling government. I was very worried about the future then. At just thirteen or fourteen years old I could feel that things were changing. I had been brought up with the sense of belonging to a village and a country I loved. Even I, at my young age, could sense that perhaps everything was going to change for the worse. 'Where are we heading?' I thought. I feared we were not going to get an education if war broke out. There was a strike in the school almost every day.

To make matters worse the local student movement had started in the cities. We heard that terrible things were happening and that some of the politics students had influenced all the students at the colleges and some in high school to go on the street and shout slogans. Everyone was being dragged into the conflict, and you could feel that law and order was going to break down. It was terrible.

The melting pot of simmering resentment between the people of the two separate Pakistani political parties, burst into violence in spring of 1971. On 25 March 1971 an East Pakistan political party called the Awami League won an election only to have the result ignored by the ruling West Pakistan establishment. This injustice whipped up outrage in East Pakistan, or East Bengal as most people would have preferred to call it. There were marches and demonstrations and fast-rising political discontent, which was met with brutal suppressive force by the West Pakistan military army in what came to be termed Operation Searchlight. This was a violent crackdown by the Pakistan army in which many people were killed and injured. The Awami League leader Sheikh Mujibur

Rahman declared East Pakistan's independence as the state of Bangladesh on 26 March 1971. The Pakistan President Agha Mohammad Yahya ordered the Pakistan military to restore the Pakistani government's authority. That began the civil war, which became known as the Liberation War.

Terrible atrocities and horrendous acts of violence took place. Operation Searchlight pursued the systematic elimination of nationalist Bengali civilians, students, religious minorities and any armed personnel. The sea of refugees heading for neighbouring India was estimated at about 10 million while another 30 million were displaced from their homes. The authorities annulled the results of the 1970 elections and arrested Prime Minister-elect Sheikh Mujibur Rahman.

There were extensive military operations and air strikes across East Pakistan as the authorities set out to suppress the tide of civil disobedience. The Pakistan army created radical religious militias, the Razakar, Al-Badr and Al-Shams, to help to stage raids on local people. Some hideous acts of violence were committed. Members of the Pakistani military and supporting militias engaged in mass murder, deportation and genocidal rape.

CHAPTER FOUR

MASSACRE

The most horrific incident I witnessed still makes me shiver every time I recall it. The Burunga massacre has gone into Bangladeshi history as one of the most savage and ruthless attacks on our people in the whole war. It was planned by the Pakistan army with ruthless cunning and carried out in Burunga of all places, a village very close to my home. The date of 26 May 1971 is well known by many Bangladeshis; it can never be forgotten. Tension began to build the afternoon before, on May 25, in Burunga and surrounding villages, because of the arrival of many Pakistani soldiers. At four o'clock in the afternoon they met with the local council union chairman and after the meeting it was announced by the beating of drums in Burunga and other nearby communities that the next morning a peace committee would be formed and 'peace cards' would be distributed from the grounds of Burunga High School, the school I myself attended.

There was great fear about what would happen and I watched the whole incident from some high ground quite a distance away. Residents of Burunga and nearby villages began gathering at the high school from eight o'clock in the morning the next day. There were around a few hundred people there by nine o'clock. That was when two well-known local men arrived in a jeep at the school grounds along with a Pakistan army contingent led by a captain. They checked the attendance against a list they had with them and seemed satisfied. Meanwhile, another group of soldiers was going from door to door in the village commanding all males to assemble in the school grounds. At around 10am the soldiers separated the group of people into Hindus and Muslims. The Hindus were herded into the office room and the Muslims were taken into a classroom inside the school building. The Muslims were ordered to individually recite the kalma and the Pakistani national anthem and after doing that most of them were allowed to go. Some left but the remaining Muslims were ordered to tie up the Hindus with ropes in groups of four. Most of the Hindus were highly educated people – doctors, judges, teachers, lawyers and civil servants. Some of the Hindus were crying with fear by now. Meanwhile, one of the captive Hindus had managed to open one of the windows and along with the headmaster of the school and a youth they jumped out of a window and ran off. I watched from my hiding place and the Pakistan army opened fire on these terrified unarmed men, but they all seemed to escape with their lives.

Watching from my hideout this was terrible to witness, but tragically there was much worse to come. At about midday the Hindus were brought out of the school building to the grounds and ninety of them were made to stand in three columns. Then they were fired at by three soldiers carrying light machine guns. It was savage, brutal and unbelievably cruel, total, inhuman carnage. I can never erase those scenes from my eyes. I have never seen anything so dreadful in my life. Soldiers from the Pakistan army then poured kerosene over the dead bodies and set them on fire.

Even then the savagery was not over. Ram Ranjan Bhattacharya, an influential lawyer at the Sylhet Judges Court who was being held by the Pakistani soldiers, was told he could go. As soon as he got up from his chair to leave he was shot in the back and killed! He died instantly. After the massacre a group of eight to ten collaborators, who were known to the villagers, looted some of the houses and molested some local women. The next day the Pakistan army returned to Burunga, hired some labourers and buried the burnt Hindu corpses in a pit beside Burunga High School. There was no agreement about the number of Hindus who were killed, with estimates ranging from seventy-one to ninety-four, but it remains one of the region's darkest days and one of the most shocking experiences of my life.

In that massacre a lot of educated people were deliberately targeted. When the war started many highly qualified people had come back from their jobs in the city to be with their families in the village. Most of them kept a home in the village even though they worked outside in the civil services or in the capital. During times of celebration or in the holidays they would always come home. At that time many of the high achievers came home to relax from work from the city. They came through the military checkpoints and were allowed in not knowing what was going to happen, and many of them were killed The Pakistanis deliberately collected all the talented, educated people. This is the first such violence I had ever experienced. We had no idea what was going to happen. I was half of a mile away with other young boys, and of course, like everyone else, I was frightened, absolutely terrified.

I was fourteen and a half and still studying at high school in 1971. But in spite of my young age I used to join the student movements when the protests and demonstrations began. Tension grew and when the war started there were a lot of killings and a great deal of terrible violence. Hundreds of thousands of people lost their lives. It was a terrible, terrible time. Officially the Bangladesh Liberation War lasted just over eight months, from 26 March 1971 until 16 December 1971, but the truth was many violent incidents occurred before the war broke out.

The local people in our village were completely unprepared for conflict. We were a peaceful folk who never had any experience of war. Within the village everyone was so friendly to each other. There was no crime. The idea of people stealing things was virtually unheard of and people used to sleep with the doors open at night. It was a very happy, social place. People enjoyed stage shows and put on dramas. They made lots of foods and held large barbecues. There were sporting programs: we would enjoy everything from fishing to football. When the Pakistan army came into our district it was a huge shock for everyone. Soldiers were suddenly everywhere in the area. Once they crossed the main highway, which is about one and a half miles away from our home, we were really scared.

At first the village people got together in protest. Many hundreds gathered, with some of the leaders saying, 'We have to face these people. We can't allow them to come into our village!' There was much shouting and brave talk.

We were young boys and very excited. Our weapons were bamboo sticks and whatever we had. There were hundreds of us marching in defiance and the soldiers were almost within half a mile. We were screaming and shouting slogans like 'Independent Bangladesh!' which, to be honest, we did not truly understand. The army responded by brush firing: shooting around the people and over their heads to frighten them. We were under the big tree and we could see bullets hitting the trees and ripping off leaves and branches. This was terrifying and everybody ran away. It was so shocking. We had no idea about fighting. We had no idea about how to take on an army. We had never seen anything like the machine guns and other terrible weapons they had. At that time the local force used to wear khaki short pants with a white turban and khaki safari shirt! They had no arms at all, not even a stick. They were scared of policemen. We were very innocent and totally unprepared for what was to happen.

When the fighting started it was a terrible, terrible shock to all of us. I have seen killings, and all the movement of war that displaced so many people. I have seen it with my own eyes. Because my father was not there, I had to take charge even though I was only young. My grandmother and I became in charge of the family. She was even then quite old. We were in danger and we spent a lot of time moving from one house to another because the Pakistan army was killing people.

I was thrust to the fore simply because my father was away in England. There was no choice; I had to grow up very quickly. The Pakistan army's main target were the Hindus. We were Muslims, so we were not in direct conflict with the army. But this was wartime and violence was everywhere, so everyone was in danger. Our next-door neighbours were attacked and some of them murdered. I've seen people killed in front of me, and the sight of a dead body, often lying out in public with evidence of the most horrific wounds, was commonplace. I've seen the most terrible things. I've seen genocide carried out brutally in front of me with people killed simply because of their religion. It was a desperately grim experience.

Terrible looting in many different places followed. The family house that was right next to our big farmhouse was looted by soldiers. When they left we went back to the village and I saw dead bodies near the house. It was our neighbours who had been shot. They were just killed for no reason, apart from their religion. The soldiers had taken them away from the house, taken over their home and let some of the looters in to steal everything. Then they shot our neighbours dead just because they were Hindu. It was terrible. Imagine how we felt! These were friends of ours who had done nothing wrong. Their lives were finished in the cruellest way and there were many cases like this.

I saw a lot more dead people and it troubled me deeply. Bodies were literally left lying around where they had been killed. It was unbelievably upsetting. They were often our friends or people who lived nearby who had just been living ordinary, happy lives. Most of them had been living next to us for years and years and all of a sudden they were shot, or blown up or burned to death. It made me grow up very quickly. People I used to know well were left lying there in pools of their own blood. Their children, their sons and daughters, were school friends of mine. All my life I had thought we were living in a peaceful place, but suddenly everything was torn apart through terrible, meaningless violence. Can you imagine how dreadful I felt? My mother and my grandmother were shattered and terrified that we would be next. Many, many people simply ran away to goodness' knows where and I have never seen them since. God knows where they went. Whole communities that had lived happily together for years were shattered. It was awful. Then the Liberation War started properly and that was the worst thing in my life that I have ever seen or experienced, more terror, more killing and more chaos. It was a total nightmare.

At that time I had very little knowledge about different religions so at first I could not even begin to understand what was going on. Before then it had never mattered to me who was Muslim and who was Hindu or Christian. I had friends from other faiths and never gave it a second thought. Even if we didn't pray together we could play together. We are all people, all the same. If you are fourteen you don't worry about things like what religion your friends belong to. The arrival of the Pakistani soldiers changed all that. I just thought, 'If it happens to him or her it could happen to me!'

We were so terrified we left our home three days after the Burunga massacre and became refugees for six or eight months. We headed for remote rural areas where we thought the army would not find us. My grandmother showed her strength of character and leadership qualities by simply saying, 'We must go.' The army camp was only about one and a half miles from our home and the soldiers used to come to the villages and take away women. It was so shocking. The soldiers were picking over the local women, and they took away the most beautiful ones. It was devastating for the families and terrifying for everyone. If anyone tried to protest they were killed. You cannot imagine how dreadful life was. My grandmother was right. We couldn't stay there.

Being the oldest son I was more vulnerable during the conflict, as I was now in charge of the family. We would stay with friends or relatives but we could not relax anywhere. We were trying to leave the country to join my father in Great Britain, but it was so difficult. With the Liberation War raging all normal travel plans were thrown into disarray and there were lots of regulations about when and where anyone could journey. I used to go to different places to try to make sure our documents were processed for travel. One of my father's cousins helped and so did an uncle, but they lived miles apart, which made communication very hard to organise. There was no telephone and you could not write a letter. I had to run from one village to another and one town to another with messages trying to find out where they were so I could communicate our movements, passing on information as best I could.

Sometime I used to travel by bus and there used to be a great number of army checkpoints. Soldiers would be there, checking whether there were any Hindu people, or any of the opposition fighters, Mukti Bahini, on the bus. In some villages were some who were fighting the army and there were many dangerous and violent incidents. If they discovered any Hindus they would take them out of the bus and shoot them in front of you. I saw a few dreadful incidents like this at checkpoints in Chondipul near Sylhet. The soldiers were very threatening. A few times I saw them just walk onto the bus, which was really the only form of transport, and six or eight of them would just push people from their seats and sit down. They were very arrogant and very frightening.

Sometimes, if they were feeling kinder, they would speak to people differently. Once a soldier got on a bus and said to me, 'You sit here.' They were big rough guys and I could hardly understand what he was saying because he was speaking in a different language, but I somehow grasped it because I was anxious not to annoy him. One soldier showed me his gun and even removed the magazine and then took a bullet out. You can imagine how frightened I was. He was just showing me he was in charge. I did not enjoy looking at this thing because a few days before I had seen a man take a bullet in front of me in our village. It was awful. There was just a little blood spot on his chest and at the back I saw a big hole where the bullet came out. That scared me very much and I often have the image in my head; I still remember it clearly. The difference between the entrance and exit injuries was somehow shocking and sickening. Human life was suddenly worth nothing to these soldiers. They thought nothing of taking a life. The nightmare lived with me for a long time and I used to be haunted by it. I have come to terms with it, of course, after all these years, but I will never forget.

I had my younger brothers and sister to protect. My mother and grandfather must have been terrified. My father must also have been desperately concerned, but in England there was nothing he could apart from follow the scraps of news that got through. I was happy to accept my role as messenger. It was scary at times but I had no choice if we were to find out what was happening and somehow organise our escape to Great Britain. My mother and grandmother and brothers and sister were also very frightened. Wherever we were staying, if it was night-time they would always stay quiet and out of the light. A lot of people disappeared during this time, they called it *ghoom* I suppose the people who went missing were killed or kidnapped.

As a young boy, racing from house to house carrying

messages and trying to get information, I was facing a lot of challenges. Now I think it was those very challenges that made me grow up fast. I became a real man and I had to be really daring. After surviving that, in all the activities I have been through since I have had nothing to fear. Nothing could be worse than what we faced during the war.

My grandfather always stayed at home with his housekeepers while the rest of us fled. In fact the army used to communicate with him but he was such a nice, respected old man that they left him alone.

I did what I could to keep my mother's spirits up and try to be the man of the family even though I was young. We all learned all the goodness of life from her. She taught us how to respect people, how to carry through your commitments, how not to gossip and how to become a good person. . . that was her challenge. I always appreciate the way we were taught by my mother.

Those terrifying months of endlessly moving and staying with family and friends were very hard on everyone. Constantly living in fear is a wretched way to be and I wished very much that there was more that I could do. Fortunately for us all, many relations, friends and other people we knew were very kind and we were very well treated. They felt privileged that we were there to take shelter with them and knew that we would never go and impose on them were it not for this crisis. All ordinary people were good to each other, as far as I can remember. We were all in the same situation. We moved from one house to another constantly. We would move around ten to fifteen miles every time because we had heard that the army was getting close. We were always trying to find somewhere safer.

Lots of people had their houses taken over by the army but luckily ours was not. Our family were quite neutral, we were not really strongly on either side. Maybe that was why our house was left alone. In the village nearby we didn't have any enemies living locally. If we'd had local enemies, I think they would have taken revenge through the army. Our family was well respected in the area. We had always tried to be fair and helpful to our tenants and neighbours. My father had built a reputation for taking care of other people. He liked to make sure that everyone lived in harmony. Although he was miles away in Britain we tried to live up to his reputation.

The aftermath of these dreadful events is still felt in my homeland today. In Bangladesh nowadays people are living in harmony, we are a peaceful nation. The chief justice in Bangladesh is now a Hindu, Mr Surendra Kumar Sinha, and if you look at most of the top Bangladeshi people they don't have that kind of discrimination that comes from outside influences. In my early years Pakistani interests dominated those of Hindus, but the Bangladeshi people were always happy to live among different religions. Today it is clear that the justice system of Bangladesh has a long memory. It has pursued some of the people who committed crimes when I was a boy. Even last year someone was hanged for murders committed many years ago. Justice is very important to the people of Bangladesh.

At the time of the Liberation War I used to pray when I had to travel through the checkpoints. I always had to make sure that I could prove I was a Muslim. Imagine being a young boy and facing a huge Pakistan army man with a machine gun shouting, 'You pray!' They made me repeat a Muslim prayer. This happened quite a few times and each time it was terrifying. If you were Muslim and you didn't say the prayer correctly, they would still shoot you. I was there once on a bus and saw them take some men out and shoot them. They took them behind rocks and killed them. We just heard the shots and it was chilling. You don't look back and you don't sympathise. That's the worst thing.

In my life now, the worst memories of this come back when I drive up to certain checkpoints where it is compulsory to stop the car. It's like a documentary of the Second World War in Germany. If the soldiers were suspicious they took everyone out looking for the enemy of their kind. This was a normal procedure, you know you have to go through the camps in Sherpur, but the worst thing is you suddenly see twelve soldiers stopping your bus in the middle of the road and you don't know what is going to happen. There may be a beautiful woman in the bus and they will drag her out or pull four people out and shoot them. That was the worst thing in life that I ever went through. I believe that after going through that nothing can really phase me. I have already faced the worst challenges in life. Nothing can be more dangerous.

But it was the massacre itself which was the worst. We could see everything and yet we could do nothing. It was a terrible, terrifying time, you couldn't judge exactly who they were killing, but we feared we would be next. Although we were Muslim and not Hindu, much of the violence was out of control and indiscriminate. Everyone was scared for their lives. The normal rules of law and order were forgotten and no one knew who would suffer next.

Our local family doctor was killed in that massacre. He was my grandmother's best friend. Two doctors died in the massacre. We all cried and wondered, 'Where are we going to go if we are sick?' It was such a terrible crime, to have people herded together and killed. The two religions, Muslim and Hindu, had got on together perfectly well for many years before this atrocity. We were like one family, there was a mosque and there was a temple. Nobody complained. I think people were more civilised and understanding when I was young. We were more respectful of our community, our religion and the beliefs of other people than we are today!

Some of the older boys went to join up to fight against the Pakistan army. At one point I wanted to enlist also. I even went to the border to try to become a fighter and one of my uncles, who was only two or three years older than, shouted to me, 'Go back.' I was literally at the border just about to enter India to get training and arms and come back and fight. I was fourteen and a half and I was going to India to enlist! When my uncle shouted I thought, 'I can't leave my family. My father is not there so I cannot be away as well. At least if I am here I can be of some use.' I just couldn't bring myself to leave my family. I went back and we kept on moving to the houses of different relatives and friends.

It was very difficult to get any proper information about what was happening. Far away in Britain my father was very worried of course, as he heard alarming news reports about what was happening in our country. He mainly had to rely on our letters to hear we were safe, although sometimes we were able to get in touch by telephone. Unfortunately the service was very unreliable. My father sent some money to help us and he called a few people, one of them quite a prominent man, to see if we could come and join him in England. I tried to be the man of the family and look after everyone, and sometimes I used to go to this gentleman's office in the city to take the telephone calls. This was not easy because I had to go through many checkpoints.

It turns out the Burunga massacre was carefully planned in advance, which somehow makes it seem even more evil to me. The soldiers organised it as away of getting rid of a lot of the senior Hindu people in the area. It was chillingly ruthless and inhuman and it still revolts me today. But it is a common story in any kind of war that terrible deeds were organised by collaborators. This was the case at Burunga. People from that same community were secretly cooperating with the army. It is sickening to think that our local people trusted them. They said they had come to our villages to talk about peace and all the good people came out thinking, 'Oh yes we need peace.' They came out with the hope of helping peace and the collaborators did their job and pointed out all the Hindu leaders, who were then shot.

As I said, years later, long after the country had become independent, justice is still closing in on some of the culprits. In many ways it is all not that long ago. When I see on the TV news now that terrorists are forcing people to prove they a member of a particular religion to avoid being brutally murdered it strikes a frightening chord inside me. It is terrible to think this is still going on. Personally, I don't want to prolong the agony of our history and keep seeking retribution for the sins of the past. I think we should just move forwards and concentrate on building a better future. Taking revenge and stirring up bad memories is not good. It should remain as part of our history, but not be part of our lives going forward. I believe the facts should all be available in the library, so if anybody wants to study the history they can go and find out for themselves. But I also believe that hatred should be allowed to calm down, and over time be completely forgotten.

The massacre and the aftermath of violence was a shocking lesson in life. It made me tough and it made me grow up. Somebody made a comment to my father long after this period that I was never afraid of anything. The truth is I had no choice at the time and had to face up to the awful atrocities going on around me. I knew then that afterwards nothing could ever be as bad.

CHAPTER FIVE

FLIGHT TO ENGLAND

It took a lot of bravery to get through the period from May 1971, when the Burunga massacre took place until, 19th October 1971 of the same shocking year, when my mother, my brothers and sister and myself finally managed to get a flight to Britain to be with my father. Many people were trying to get out of the country any way they could and it was very difficult to get the tickets, but my family knew some quite influential people who helped us a lot. My father's nephew and his uncle and other relatives also offered a great deal of help. My father had been communicating by telegram with them. He paid them the money. All I had to do was to go and sit down in his office hour after frustrating hour waiting for him to call me. Eventually the call came through, we had the tickets and at long last the trip was on! It was very exciting. My grandparents put us on the plane as they wanted to stay behind.

We were all crying. It was one of the saddest moments in my

young life to leave my grandparents. It was a very emotional parting. My grandmother gave me a great big hug and a smile full of assurances. There were tears in their eyes but I also saw relief. My grandfather was very fond of England. He made flying visits when he was in the merchant navy whenever their ship docks. He knew that it is a safe country. Deep inside I knew we were going to a better place. A country that offers a lot of opportunities.

We could afford the flights, although the tickets were very expensive, but of course money isn't important when it comes to the safety of your family. We flew with the Pakistan International Airline (PIA) from Dhaka to Karachi. Then there were problems and we were stuck in Karachi for a few days trying to sort things out. We called our father and he helped, and eventually we got a flight on to Bahrain, and then eventually another to London Heathrow!

I will never forget the excitement and elation I felt at that moment of our arrival. My father was there waiting for us and it was wonderful to see him. I was so proud to see him in his suit and tie, looking like a real gentleman. He'd been in England for five years by then. We knew he had a good house, a job and quite a decent standard of living. I think out of the group of men he came to Britain with, he was the first one to buy a house. And at first one or two of his friends lived there with him for a time. I was so happy to see him. He was my hero

We all felt such amazing relief. I had seen and experienced a lot of terrible things, but seeing my father at the airport in London, I knew we had come safely through it all. The whole experience had been an ordeal for all of us, terrifying for us of course, but also for my father who had been anxiously awaiting news. We had all been through a whirlwind of change. Our family had been respected and successful for many generations then was suddenly on the run in fear of our very existence, living as fugitives moving from house to house. But we are very positive people, and to some extent, arriving in Great Britain was not all bad. We began to see it as more of an opportunity than a disaster if we looked at the potential of living in safety in a thriving new country.

We had members of the family in many countries. Relatives had settled in Canada, England, Italy and in other countries, because after the war, Bangladesh was left in a very sorry state. When the country gained independence it had nothing. Pakistan did not give Bangladesh anything. They had taken so much. They even took all the planes and destroyed the bridges and much of the infrastructure. So Bangladesh started from a very, very poor base. It took so many years, a few decades even, to recover from that. If we had remained in Bangladesh, we would have struggled a lot and been much poorer. Leaving our homeland was terrifying and dangerous, but overall I think it was a great opportunity and the best thing that could have happened to us.

Once we were on the plane, certainly it was a massive relief. Most of the family members also flew out. They realised it was not a place to live any more and most of them that could travel took the decision to leave. A lot of people had died and it was a great opportunity for us, and I think our children should appreciate what we did. They were not born in Bangladesh. They were born here in Britain. I see the best side of any situation. I could moan, but I much prefer to look for the good in everything. I think that is one of my strengths. Life has to go on. You can't just go on grumbling and complaining about the misfortunes of the past and going through bad memories and poor legacy. It is not positive. You have to look on the bright side – I am one of the world's optimists!

There is the other side of the story, which I hear from some of my friends who stayed in Bangladesh. Some of them became successful there. They took the opposite point of view, saying, 'We are not going anywhere. We want to build the country back up again.' They became strong nationalists, some of them campaigning politicians. They took on the challenge and opportunity of rebuilding the country. That is another side to what happened and I deeply respect them for it. But I do not regret leaving, which we did for the best, and I am sure it was the right decision for us.

Before the war our childhood life was good. In fact, looking back, it was more than good; it was idyllic. It was far from a rich country, and when you are poor your people don't get good welfare support. Numbers were growing fast and over twenty or thirty years the population more than doubled. In 1974 the population of Bangladesh was 76 million and now it's almost 160 million. For a long time the people were not well looked after or well educated, but now, as the economy improves, people are more educated and much better off. Health education and welfare has massively improved. Birthrate is controlled. After all the struggles, especially for independence, but also to make life more comfortable and happy, to improve the healthcare system and provide free education to everyone, Bangladesh has a bright future. I'm happy that Seamark has a big part to play in that.

When we made our flight to what we saw as freedom and a fresh start we had no idea what would happen. We couldn't have dreamed of how it has all eventually turned out. We just thought, 'Thank goodness we're all still alive'. I came here to Great Britain and didn't go back home to Bangladesh until nine years later. But in those nine years I felt constant love and affection for Bangladesh because my memories were always with me. After that, now I have settled down here, I feel more comfortable being with my family. But during the first five or six years, or even up to the time I went back, I really felt for that country because my childhood had been there and it was still my home in my heart. My childhood friends were there and I had all the memories of growing up, and playing, and all the fields I played football, cricket and all the other games in. There were many difficult times, with natural disasters like flooding, but they did not affect the area we lived in. There were lots of problems in starting a new nation, but many of them were to be expected and were eventually solved.

When we first arrived in Great Britain we spent one day in London and then my father took us by train to Oldham, where by then he had a two-bedroom terraced house. We did not know quite what to expect from England. Communicating only by letter and telegram for five years made it so hard not only for my father to get news from Bangladesh but also for us to learn about life in England. We didn't know what to expect. But coming from the hot sunshine and lovely countryside of Bangladesh my first reaction was that the wet and cold streets of terraced houses in Oldham did not look too appealing.

Bangladesh is a beautiful, bright country full of sunshine and lots of greenery. Every day you see stunning sunrises and sunsets. You don't praise the weather in our country. You tend to take it for granted. It is always good unless it's raining. Monsoon is the worst time, otherwise it's lovely most of the year round. However, we were made very welcome in Oldham. My father's friends were very kind and generous.

When we arrived there wasn't a big family reunion, but my father had lots of friends and they came round to greet us. We were one of the first Bangladeshi families to move into Oldham and we were made to feel very special. We were given cash and taken to the houses of my father's friends and very well looked after. I remember people giving us money and giving us sweets. It was not just Bangladeshis, but Indian people, and Polish and Ukrainians: immigrants like to get together far from home. My father took me to a store called Lewis's and this friend of his bought me two or three shirts. We had a fantastic time. It was very exciting, particularly for the first few days.

Unfortunately, once we had settled in, I found that life in Oldham was far from fantastic. I was shocked to find there was no bathroom in our house, only a toilet that was outside. I mean, when I first came to Britain I used to go to the public baths with my father. One after the other we would line up with other men for a shower. Life was very different. Where we lived there were no cars on the street – though nowadays you can't find a car park space anywhere!

To be honest, when I first came to Britain, even though I was delighted for the family to be safely reunited with my father in the house in Oldham, my immediate surroundings did not exactly thrill me. It was great for the family to be together again, thousands of miles from the fighting and the killings, but in late October I was very unhappy to see how miserable and grey and foggy Oldham appeared to be. And it was a bit of a shock to find my new home was a small terraced house. In high school we had learned a lot about the history of Great Britain. We had learned about the beautiful houses and grand buildings and had dreams of Buckingham Palace and the Houses of Parliament in our minds. Our new surroundings were rather different. Oldham seemed to be very grey and full of small houses with lots of people working like machines morning to night in the factories and the foundries. There were even more grey people working in the mill, where my father had his job.

It seemed to be always raining there was no sunshine. Everybody seemed to work regular round-the-clock shifts in the mill. They worked from 6am until 2pm, 2pm until 10pm, and 10pm until 6am. Although I didn't know it at the time this was in fact the end of the heyday of the mills, but they were still grinding people down in those days. You did not see any success stories, and there weren't any successful Asian people. Everybody was in the same category. The country did not even seem that rich. Britain appeared dependent on these lowly mill workers and I knew from the very start that I never wanted to join their ranks.

I had lots of role models when I was a child, but there were not many businessmen among them and I always wanted to be a businessman. When I arrived in England my father instantly became my role model. He was quite an impressive man. He worked for only a few years in the mill and then took redundancy and with that he bought his three properties.

Our original house when we came in to England was number 3 Landseer Street in Oldham. Today my house in Wilmslow is also called The Landseer, in memory of that first address, and of my father of course. He worked very hard to try to look after us all when we arrived but it was not easy for him. And then after he had got some money from his redundancy he bought a shop and a house next door from one of his friends. That was numbers 12 and 14, Sickle Street, Oldham. We expanded the shop into 14 and later housed all the cold storage there! He used to run that shop, but he was not particularly successful. Sadly, by then his health was not so good; he was not a well man.

There were not many Bangladeshis or even Asian people who had the kind of vision my father had in those days. Unfortunately Richard Branson and people like him were not around then or I would have perhaps been inspired by someone more modern! My father always helped me. Whatever I wanted he tried to help me and he gave me the opportunities. He was a very, very generous man to many people and particularly to me. He never said no. Later it was different, and I was the one who never said no, but that was after many years. He was my idol and I always admired him.

I don't mean to be rude or unkind to the country that took us in, but it was grim in those first months. I was unhappy.

CHAPTER SIX

LONDON

I tried to get into the school but I couldn't get a place. The law said that after you reached the age of fifteen you could not get into school for free. I was too old at fifteen and a half, so my father couldn't put me in the ordinary school. I couldn't go to school unless my father paid fees and sent me to private school, which would have cost a lot of money. My father could not afford that. Plus, I needed language training to learn English. At the time I could only speak the little I had learned in school in Bangladesh. One of my uncles who lived in London – in fact he was my father's second cousin – said to my father, 'Well, send him to my place. We have a lot of night schools in London, he can do English classes.' It was good advice. There was much more going on down there than in Oldham.

So I went to London and this is where I started evening school. It was the best decision for me. I was nearly sixteen and I needed to study and to learn English, besides which, after about four or five months in Oldham, I was very bored. I had heard so much about London. I don't think my father really wanted me to leave the family, but he said, 'If you want to go to London, you can go.' I didn't really know what to do. I had no friends in this strange new country. There was just one family contact in the capital, which was very fortunate for me. I went to live with my relative, Joynal Abedin. He was older than me and was working. He encouraged me to study. Language was my biggest problem as my spoken English wasn't too good. So I went to night school to improve it.

That was a great move, because I found a lot of new friends who had also come from Bangladesh and who were in same situation. I did the course for about two and a half years. I was also trying to find a job to support myself. I've done all sorts of jobs I didn't like; I have never been frightened of hard work. But to begin with, in the daytime for months I didn't do anything. After a while I found work in a community centre, a warehouse, a shop. Then I found some more, very different, jobs.

At first I wasn't too unhappy with this relative in East London. My father's second cousin was a great man and he treated me very well. It was a small flat with two bedrooms and four of us lived there; I used to share a room. It was not an easy way of life, in fact it was very tough. I never had much money, so cash was always a problem. Very generously they didn't charge me anything for rent for the first six months. For two and a half years I did night school to get my English up to scratch.

It was expensive to study. I had to buy so many things.

My father never wanted to make us feel short of anything, so whenever I returned to Oldham, he used to take me shopping and buy me the famous 'K' shoes. He always felt it was important that you were wearing good shoes. I agreed with that one hundred per cent, as appearance is very important, but I felt bad because I knew he was really struggling because of all the money it had cost to bring us to England. He always insisted on buying me good shoes even when I said they were too expensive. It was very difficult and upsetting. Also, my two brothers and my sister all needed looking after. I remember my father took enrolled them in the best school in Oldham and he had to buy the uniforms, the books, the bags and everything else they needed. In those days, uniforms were the best and very expensive. He was running short of money but he would never let us know that. He was a very proud man.

I was not always happy in London, but I always loved the capital city. It was a very memorable time in my life because I was away from my family. That meant that I went through some very sad times for four or five years. I was often left feeling very lost and lonely. Your late teens and early twenties are an age when you should be having a good time, and gradually, after a few years, I managed to make lots of friends. My life really cheered up when I had friends to go out with to the theatre and to the cinema almost every weekend, and also to study with at night school. My favourite films were: *The Magnificent Seven, Papillion, The Great Escape, Zulu, Dirty Harry*, and *Smokey and the Bandit*. I liked Steve McQueen, Burt Reynolds, Charles Bronson, James Coburn, John Wayne, Michael Caine, Gene Hackman and Kirk Douglas.

After I had completed the education courses I attended City College, Westminster and did lots of business management courses at and obtained business diplomas. My childhood ambitions remained unchanged: I still intended to be a businessman. I never wanted to work for someone else. I was always determined to run a business for myself. Since I was a little boy I had decided that I would create some kind of a business and make it grow. That was always my dream. I aimed to be somebody. Even when I was very, very young, as young as I can remember, I had the vision that this was what I would do with my life.

After staying in East London with my cousin, I later moved to Paddington where I lived for three years. For almost six years I lived in London. I did many different courses and earned my diploma in management. I wanted to go to university but decided it would probably be a waste of time. I didn't really fancy the idea of doing any more studies. My early life in London was really challenging. When my father left Bangladesh I was very young. I tried to be responsible and to do everything for the family, for my brothers, sister and mother. Now in London I knew it was time to learn and to better myself. I was trying to study but it was not an easy time. There was much trouble, lots of industrial action and strikes. It was a recession and people were migrating to other countries. I thought of going to Australia but I could not leave my family.

CHAPTER SEVEN

RACISM

England was such a completely different environment from Bangladesh. For a time I was not happy. In Bangladesh I was able to see a good future, in spite of all the conflict we had experienced. There I could see what I might achieve, but it took me quite a long time to work out what I might achieve in the UK.

At this time in London there was a lot of violent racism. This was the time of skinheads and their violent attacks, and of Enoch Powell's inflammatory speeches being endlessly quoted. In many ways, for a young Asian man in London these were terrible times. I was not so much frightened for myself as frustrated about my hopes for the future. What can I do for my family here? I thought. I knew I couldn't go back to Bangladesh. I was worried that I would never even get a job, or a proper start in life. We got a lot of abuse from the wrong sort of white people! Every day my Bangladeshi friends and I would face swearing and hear men shouting at us, 'Black bastard, go back home!' And often it was, 'Paki go back home', which was harsh as well as darkly ironic when you consider it was Pakistani violence that we had fled from in order to try to find safety in the UK. For quite a time life was scary and unpleasant. We were pushed around on the Tube and threatened on the street. It was terrible.

Memories can be softened and mellowed by time, but the truth is that racism was a daily nightmare. Every time I went to night school, I got abuse. I took different routes to avoid the boys who were shouting at me and waiting for me. Slowly we realised it was happening to all of us, so three of us immigrant friends used to try and stick together. Then one day a gang attacked us and there was a fight. There were six or seven of them and three or four of us. We lost and it was very painful. We could not communicate properly because we could not speak English. All the Asian people kept together and we lived in a ghetto; we didn't go to the pub. We knew we were different and we had no command of the English language. Perhaps they were frightened of these strange people who came to their country. They said we were taking their jobs and houses, and attacked with broken bottles. Many times they attacked us and we would be hurt, people were bleeding and injured. Me and my friends even went to kung fu classes to learn self-defence. A few of us joined a campaign against racism and met up with leaders and attended organised demonstrations.

There was much talk of a great shortage of housing. Everyone seemed to live in a council flat and they saw Asians and immigrants from other countries getting them and thought we were stealing their houses. They could not see how much contribution Asian people could make to society.

Often we were in a group because we felt a little safer that way. We never wanted to attack anybody, but we felt we must not run away from a fight. 'Why are you fighting?' we used to ask as we tried to protect ourselves. After the fight we would still say, 'Why are you shouting at us? We have done nothing wrong.' They would say, 'It's not me, it's my mates.' We would try to reason with them but it was hopeless. Many times it happened, but we never attacked, we just defended. At times this violent racism made me consider returning to Bangladesh but I always knew that you couldn't let thugs win. Many people were kind to us and it would have cost us a lot of money to go back to Bangladesh, and where was I going to go anyway? My family was here in England.

Once there were three of us 'Pakis', as the racists always called us. In fact we were two Bangladeshis and a Kenyan Indian! We went to this Irish pub in London, just three friends having a night out. The singer David Essex used to come in sometimes because his auntie worked in the pub. We bought a drink and sat down and we were talking to some girls. Suddenly this guy, a complete stranger, just came up and said, 'Get out of this place. We don't want you here.' One of the girls screamed really loudly at him. She was a friend of ours and she was very angry and she shouted, 'We are just sitting here minding our own business. Who are you to tell us to go!' But we did not want to have a scene, or a fight, or trouble of any kind. We said, 'Look it is best we go.' We just left our drinks and went. It was awful. We were so embarrassed, and the three girls were so upset.

There were so many similarly rough people wanting to make trouble out of nothing. And many years later that was the sort of thing I didn't want my children to have to experience. So

I would always try to protect them. I think the young Asian people of today should appreciate what older people have done for them in Britain. It has improved greatly now, but we went through a lot for our right to remain in this country. Racism is evil. Everybody should get on well together.

Of course, it's not just in Britain. People everywhere in the world are racist. It is natural for people with a nationality in common to group together. Anything or anyone different is a threat. The clashes of violence were nothing unexceptional, it happens all over the world. When I was in London I was someone most people didn't understand and I was living in their country. We couldn't speak English properly and they turned on us. I liked to live with my friend because he could speak English and we lived close to the Asian grocery shop. If I went to an English area I didn't know what language I was supposed to speak.

I was attacked many times in London, often by the dreaded skinheads. I saved myself many times simply by running away. I controlled myself. I have always been very calculating and wherever I went I always tried to leave myself an escape route. I don't lose control when I am confronted by difficulty. I manage things carefully. With the skinheads, I always thought first, 'Should I go this way or that way. Who am I going to face?' It is better to be careful and choose the safest way out. I never wanted to get into any trouble; I tried to stay out of it.

But I am not bitter about those attacks. It could happen to anybody. I always felt that I am from Bangladesh and I am in their country, so I must behave properly. There are Asian people now claiming, 'I am part of England.' Of course you are part of England, but you have to prove yourself. You cannot just come from another country and claim yourself to be British – you have to prove you can live and behave properly before you can expect to be accepted. If you want to be seen and accepted as a good citizen of this country then you have to make a contribution. You cannot just come here and take the benefits and not put anything back into this country. I think that is wrong, it is not good.

A lot of English people became very good friends with us. I firmly believe that, even back then, for the majority of people it did not really matter what colour your skin was. The only reason Asian people became established here is I think because we have a relationship with British people as they ruled us for so many years. Bangladeshi people have a respect for the Britishness in our characters, which is why we could easily adjust with the British people. Many things about the Bangladeshi way of life sees us doing things the British way, in terms of language, in terms of respecting each other and showing courtesy. But there are communities who don't see that and there are the minority who are racist, and unfortunately there will always be people like that.

I think my time in my home in East London's Tower Hamlets was the lowest period for me. I was frustrated and I was sad. I was struggling with language, and very unhappy. Later I moved to Paddington, which was a better place. My first job was in Liverpool Street, just helping in an office doing odd jobs. I always knew it was not only me who suffered racist abuse. We were a group of people who were unjustly persecuted. At times we were exploited by politicians but overall, I believe, we were sensible and did not try to get any revenge.

We did find some fine people who stood up for us. One of the teachers introduced us to a volunteer called Peter East, a night-school teacher and social worker who used to get funds to do good works and he helped us a lot. Peter East was such a nice man, an older guy who helped me and other Bangladeshi children enormously. He lived at the Tower Bridge complex where he was in charge and did volunteer work. He was a teacher and a social worker and he helped me and other Bangladeshi children a lot. He used to run a guesthouse where I stayed for a few weeks, and when we had this racism problem and we wanted to protect ourselves, he offered us a basement. It was a kind of gym. He kitted us out with equipment such as boxing gloves and a punch bag. We did not really want to fight anyone; we were simply training to protect ourselves. He used to take us to Brighton to the seaside and organised many trips and visits to places such as museums, universities and historical sites. We had a lot of fun and learned how to associate with other communities. There were a lot of Bangladeshi kids but there were kids from all over the world. We learned about Great Britain and helped to deal with the British way of life and people. It was a very inspirational time.

There were many good English people, who helped us and were kind; the racists were a minority. There was a lady called Miss Ferguson who spent many years with us guiding and teaching us. So there was a positive side as well as the negative side. And there was another man, also called Peter who spoke fluent Bangladeshi. He was kind to us as well. They were the nicest people, some of my teachers, Jennifer, Christine. . . they were the people who influenced me greatly to become a better man. They were decent people who lifted our spirits greatly when we were being persecuted. They didn't see us as immigrants; they didn't see us as people who came from a poor country. They just thought we were nice people who could do as well as anybody else. They taught us things that I still remember.

For years I was angry that I couldn't get on, I regretted being here, but I had no choice. Even after Bangladesh became independent, the country was not doing well. There were many shortages and the people suffered terrible floods and shortages of food. I knew I couldn't go back. My family was here and I steeled myself to succeed in the UK. Deep down I refused to let the racism bother me. I knew the majority of English people were nice people. I very rarely went to pubs. Sometimes we went to a disco club as well as the cinema every week. That was the best entertainment you could find when you weren't spending money on drinking. I met a girl who became a friend, but she was not really a girlfriend. It was all quite innocent.

There were very tough times, but it was not all bad. I loved the energy and liveliness of London. There were lots of parties and young people having a good time. I had many different jobs because you always need money in London. At one time I used to work for a drama company, helping to put on a lot of stage shows, some at the Phoenix Theatre. I was young and at times I was attracted to finding a glamorous job, but at the end of the day money is more important. I made quite a few visits back to Oldham to see my family and the news was not good there. The family faced a growing cash crisis.

My father had left his job in the mills by this time, and started to run the grocery shop, but it was not a great success. In spite of this shortage of money I somehow managed to keep up a very good lifestyle. I always travelled first class and I always wore nice branded clothes and ate in nice restaurants. I always like the best and usually I had the best. Somehow this was managed even though the family didn't have much money. My father was supporting me in those days, so later when I found out he couldn't really afford it I felt really bad.

CHAPTER EIGHT

BACK TO OLDHAM

After about six years the attraction of London began to wear off. A lot of the friends I made at that time got married and settled down and suddenly I didn't see them again. There were not so many parties and I suppose I began to grow up. Finding a job was difficult and life became lonely. I had enjoyed my life in London but I knew that my father and my family needed me back in Oldham and after quite a few visits, I considered moving back permanently to look after my family. I was very torn between London and Oldham for a time.

In 1977 my father developed diabetes and he also suffered from water in his lungs because he was a heavy smoker. He was a very sick man for a time and sometimes he was unable to work. This increased the pressure on me to return home to Oldham to help the family. We were one of the first Bangladeshi families in Oldham, but we were quickly followed by quite a few more families who moved into the area. By the mid-1970s there were quite a lot of us, I suppose. Other friends helped my father but I still felt the weight of responsibility.

I mentioned earlier that my father bought a house and a shop in Sickle Street. I should explain here that the way my father acquired the shop was somewhat less than straightforward. It happened after one of his friends, a man called Kotai Miah, borrowed money from my father and found he could not pay it back on time. 'Buy my shop!' he said. My father was not at all keen on the idea at first and replied, 'Why do I want to buy a shop?' Kotai Miah said, 'It's an investment. If you give me more money than the cost of my debt you can have it.' My father decided he wanted the shop, but he wanted my opinion, too. I had grown up and he asked me what he should do. I encouraged him to take the shop. It was not something he had planned to do, but it seemed like a good prospect. That is how it happened. The shop was running OK for a while but in the end it proved otherwise.

The grocery shop was still in the family when I was thinking of returning, but although I was not clear exactly where my future lay I knew I never wanted to work in it. I was frustrated. When I visited, my father was not well and the business was in a lot of debt. My mother used to call me up on the telephone and say, 'Your father is not well. He's in the hospital.' She was upset and worried. My young brother Kamal was having to take more and more leave from college to run the shop. He used to rush back and go straight behind the counter. This was not right. He was quite young and his education was suffering. There was a cash crisis, which meant no one in the house was happy. So what should I do? First, I went back to London because I was more comfortable there, but when I returned, although I still had one or two very close pals who were not married and settled down, I started to realise everything had changed. Then my conscience pricked and I thought about my family.

Even then, as inexperienced as I was, I knew that any business you start, you cannot have a huge income from it from the first moment. Unfortunately my father needed a huge income because he had four children. With a big family it was expensive to live, even in those days. My father had to buy a colour TV. He had to buy a car. Everybody wanted pocket money to go to the cinema. The cash crisis was always there. The income from that shop was not too bad at the start, but it soon proved to be not enough. Slowly, slowly he borrowed money and took more credit from people. This is where he became financially vulnerable and this was when I came into the business. The shop was losing money and I had to clear some of his debts.

My father was a wonderful man, so kind and caring and he would do anything for his family. He was a very calming influence on us all. Even when things weren't going too well he would still appear very relaxed and just say, 'Take it easy.'

So I decided to come back. I made the decision in 1977, but I wavered a great deal to be honest, and it was not until 1978 that I finally went back to Oldham for good. It took me a long time to decide because I really loved London. I still love London

In the end I had no choice. I went to Oldham to help run the shop because I knew it was my duty to the family. But I also knew that running a small shop was not my kind of business. I wanted something with real potential. 'This is not

my business,' I told my mother. I wanted to run some kind
of business, but I was interested in something bigger, much
bigger, than this shop. For me everything has to be bigger. I
have always been very ambitious. My dreams were always
bigger than anybody else's. How was I going to achieve this?
I was not at all sure.

When I came back, I think for about a year I was not quite
sure whether I was going to stay or go back to London. I
thought Oldham was miserable. You can imagine how it felt
coming from the bright lights of London to the gloom and
grime of Oldham. I used to go to see films in the Odeon,
Leicester Square. I came north and went to the Odeon in
Oldham. It didn't match by a mile. And I had left all my good
teenage friends in London, so in that first year back I made at
least twelve trips to London to visit friends. I used to go for the
weekend when most people would not have done something
so extravagant. My father was still very generous and he gave
me pocket money during this time so I was able to go out
and have a life. I was very undecided about where my future
really lay. My older friends were mostly already married or
thinking about it, and a good friend said to me, 'Go back to
your family and do something.'

But gradually I started to take control of the business
even though I never really worked in the shop. If you have a
business and you build up debts, it's a big problem. It was in
debt from the start, and I was thinking hard about what to
do. I wanted to do something better, something with more
potential. I decided there was more future in wholesale than
retail and I told my brother Kamal: 'Look I am not going
behind the counter. You stay there and I will stay out and do
the purchases for you. You just sell the products.'

At this point my father gave me some very strong and valuable support. Dad said to the family, 'Look here, Iqbal is leading and we must all follow him, respect him and listen to what he says.' That was the best recommendation that I could have wished for. That made me the family leader. It was partly because I was the most go-ahead and partly because I was the oldest. It is our tradition to follow the oldest brother's lead. Our belief is that if you don't respect the oldest brother you don't live harmoniously and you never become successful. As well as my dad, equal credit should go to my mother. She told my younger brothers, 'Right, whatever Iqbal says is right! Follow his leadership!' Of course I would discuss all my plans with my parents. We would then discuss them with my brothers and then I used to implement them.

Meanwhile, even in Oldham the racism was also very bad at times. There were always people waiting to attack you and plenty of no-go areas for Asians. Anywhere near the Waterloo Street Bridge was definitely one of them. Skinheads were a constant threat for a time. However, I was determined to stay and make a go of it in Oldham in spite of everything. The family is more important than the individual. That is really why I came back from London. I tried to think of something different and good for my future. I always think big. I never think small. I never copy anyone because I always like to go my own way. I like to do something very niche, something different. I had many friends in Oldham in the textiles business. I attempted to break into that world many times, but somehow it did not happen. The garments industry did not work out for me. My father had done well in getting promoted and I thought there might be a future for me there, too. I had a dream of setting up my own textile mill in Bangladesh, taking machines over there from English mills, but somehow it didn't work out.

When you have no money in business you have to start doing something pretty quickly. So I got myself involved with the shop and started to supply produce to local restaurants. But the shop was no good for me and I had no money to work with, so I started to think about borrowing money to do something different. In those days Bangladeshi so-called Indian restaurants were opening all over the UK. They were springing up like mushrooms. I thought wholesaling food to the new restaurants could be the basis of a very good business. I could see the potential of the catering industry.

To get started with my business dreams I needed capital. I had very little and so I went to my father's friends. 'Look I need money,' I said. 'I will pay you back. I have decided to stay here, I am going to work hard and try to build a business.' They were very good to me. They trusted me and agreed to loan me the money I needed to get started. They were not rich people. I don't think all of them even had even bank accounts!

These good people used to work hard and they didn't know what to invest their money in. 'Well give it to me, I'll give it you back on time,' I said.. To be honest, I was so well known and well thought of locally that many people used to offer money to me. I made sure I always paid them back on time. That helped to give me a better cushion.

People from Bangladesh have a great respect for the older generation, more perhaps than people from other countries do. I still have uncles and cousins that I make sure I talk to on a regular basis. This is why I enjoy my success. When I meet my father's friends, they give me some feeling about my father. That is part of the strength of our community. When

I started it was my father's friends who gave me a salary every week, they really helped just when I needed it. They never questioned, never doubted and always supported. Everything I have achieved since then was started with the help of their generosity. Without them, who knows what might have happened.

Whenever I wanted to borrow more money it was no problem, honestly. Because they were all bachelors and they worked six days a week, they couldn't go to the bank and they couldn't spend it. They knew I needed money and they helped me so much. I think it helped because I was always honest and I always extended my help to the community of friends. That is the reputation I built from my childhood. They must have seen something in me and my ambitious plans. Sometimes I have to work hard to control myself. I still think I can do anything in life.

Fortunately, my wholesale business supplying shops and restaurants worked pretty well straight away. Almost as soon as I began trading I began turning a profit. Of course in the earliest days the margins were smaller, but I learned fast and worked hard. I could easily see where my dad's problems lay. He had accumulated lots of debts and his income was not enough to pay them; his income was not even as high as his expenses. This is why his debts were going up and up. He could not pay people on time. He was borrowing more money from the bank and he was borrowing more from his friends and relatives. Things were not working because he was still spending more than he was earning in the shop. In that situation you have to earn more or reduce your expenses otherwise you cannot survive. If you want to have more expenses, that's fine, but you have to sell three times as much in the shop or you have to reduce your expenses. It is easier to live on less, a simple calculation.

It was quite a responsibility helping my father out of that problem, which is why I have enjoyed my freedom from money worries so much ever since. When I lived in London I had a great lifestyle going to the bright lights of the West End, and then coming to Oldham experienced quite a drop in excitement. But then I thought, 'No, this is important for my family.' And I would tell myself that I had taken on a charitable job. In fact, my very first charitable job was for my own family. Again, when you do things like this it can seem as if you are doing it for others, but I believe you are also doing it for yourself. Helping other people always makes me feel good. I enjoy doing it.

CHAPTER NINE

MARRIAGE

I have made many good decisions since those early days of establishing myself as a wholesale trader in Oldham and in Manchester in the late 1970s, but the best decision I made had nothing at all to do with business. On 28 May 1978 I married a beautiful Bangladeshi lady called Salma and we have been so fortunate to enjoy a very happy marriage and produce three remarkable and dynamic children, Shahida, Manzur and Hamida.

My wife means everything to me. I am a very lucky man to have found the perfect partner in life. I do enjoy the company of women very much and loved spending time with my mother and grandmother when I was younger. Anything to do with the family I used to discuss with my mother and I do the same with my wife now. We had a traditional wedding. Our family grew up with this sort of traditional culture. My father used to sing traditional songs. There was a poet in our family and we used to enjoy all the festivals in Bangladesh. There was much singing and dancing and our neighbours were also involved. This is our culture; we sing, we dance. I always had in mind that it might be difficult to adapt to England.

You see, when I came here you hardly saw any brown-skinned people. I personally found it very difficult to form a relationship with an English girl because she might want her way and I might want my way. I was lonely when returned to Oldham, a bit frustrated. Coming back from London was an unusual thing to do. People normally travel from the village to the city, so my case was completely different. I had made a few friends and we used to go out, but places were not up to the mark, compared to London, where I went to the West End and Leicester Square or over to Kensington. I used to go to Albert Hall to listen to music and to the theatre. In Oldham you could only go to the cinema to see a film or to a club in Manchester. So I had become a bit isolated. I therefore tried to cut back on going out, and to curb my lifestyle. The time was right for me to settle down

For seven years I had enjoyed being single and growing into an adult in England, but my friends had started to get married, some of them to English girls. There were one or two girls I used to know in those days, from quite affluent Bangladeshi families, but I wasn't up to their standard.

When I arrived back in Oldham and my mother asked me if I had anybody in my life, I told her frankly I had friends but had not committed to anybody. She asked me what sort of girl I wanted to settle down with. 'A good Bangladeshi girl, if you can find one,' I replied. So they started looking and sent me pictures. Then my grandmother came out with a strong proposal, a girl from a family she knew very well. She was from a highly educated family with cultural minds, still living in Bangladesh. We met in London.

Her father used to live in England and he was a good friend of my dad. It was organised that she flew over as my fiancée. I saw her for the first time at Heathrow Airport when she came through immigration; it was surprisingly emotional and quite exciting. My father and myself were there, and my mother and one or two of her relatives. It was like a fun day when somebody comes from abroad. She was exceptional, very beautiful. She was a bit shy, I think, and didn't talk much, but I think she was pleased to see me. After a few weeks we got married in London. One of my father-in-law's nephews had a restaurant in Oxford Street, in London. We had a ceremony there in a nice, informal way.

We didn't have a honeymoon as such. We were in London and we spent a few days together there; that was our honeymoon. Our first home was back in the family home in Oldham, a small terraced house, shared with my brothers and sisters and parents. Only one sister was born before we arrived, but more were born later. Of course we had separate bedrooms.

Meeting my wife was the start of a period of great happiness and considerable relief. Marriage is a commitment for life, I always had a traditional marriage to a beautiful girl from Bangladesh in the back of my mind, and for me it has worked very well. Salma was perfect in every way and she still is today.

When I really got to know the lady who had become my wife I found we were very much on the same wavelength in every way. It was a big plus. Her heritage is from Bangladesh and she came from a very good family. We had a lot in common from the start. Her family were all very well educated and kind, respectful people. I have learned a lot from her and I think vice versa. She enjoys my company and I'm very happy with her. I found in her everything I wanted in a woman. She is cultural, she is educated, she can tell me more about Bangladesh than I know because when I came to England I was young. The magic, the chemistry between us, was very good from the start.

It was not a forced marriage. There is no forced marriage in Bangladesh. Or if there is, it is very rare. Normally it doesn't happen. An arranged marriage is not a forced marriage. My parents had an arranged marriage and they were very happy together. My mother was from a similar background to my father and they were very well suited. My parents lived with me for most of the time. Sometimes my dad lived in Bangladesh, but mostly he was in Britain with me.

In an arranged marriage like ours the parents get information about a possible partner beforehand, and help their children to find someone. It's sensible because we don't go to clubs and we don't socialise like Europeans do. Although, I am speaking more of the old days, because now they do socialise. In those days we lived a more conservative life and it was good that we came from same background. We were both in our early twenties, which I think is about the right time to get married. We were not too old and not too young. Our wedding in the restaurant in Oxford Street was a very happy occasion.

At that time I had already started the business. I think my mother especially was more sympathetic towards me. She thought that I needed to be looked after well because I worked so hard, twelve or fourteen hours a day, and I did a lot of travelling to different parts of the country. I didn't have many friends. My mother always supported me, though at first I opposed her and said I didn't think it was the right time to get married. But she was very firm and said, 'Yes I think it is the right time.' She added, 'Look, your father is thinking of going back to Bangladesh. We might go back and you will be alone, you need somebody with you to take care of you. I think this is the best time.'

She was right of course. After I got married, maybe one year later, they went back to Bangladesh. I was very happy with my wife. I want to give her the chance here to tell her side of the story. What is it like to be married to me?

CHAPTER TEN

MRS SALMA AHMED'S STORY

My husband and I came to meet because Iqbal's father and my father became friends in the UK. We lived in Bangladesh and my father came to England to study for a degree in ceramic engineering. People from Bangladesh often get together in a foreign country and my father and Iqbal's father became friends. My father was living in Congleton, which is not too far from Oldham, so they spent some time together. The family story is that my father said, 'OK, I have got a daughter. Why don't we check up on how she gets on with your son?'

I didn't know anything about this at all because I was at home in Sylhet, Bangladesh studying. My father gave Iqbal's father one picture of me. Iqbal's father had a good sense of humour and he was also very romantic. He took the picture of me with my friends, went to an artist and got him to cut out the picture of me and put it together with a picture of his son! He put them together so we looked liked a couple and said, 'Now what do you think? Your daughter and my son! How do think they look together? OK, eh?'

By then the wheels had already been set in motion for Iqbal and I to meet. Soon after the cleverly created romantic photo, my father brought me to London and we met Iqbal's father. He was very nice. At that time I was about twenty and for three or four years our fathers were talking like that. I think it was really just two good friends talking and joking about Iqbal and myself. Iqbal's father would say to my father, 'Bring your daughter in to London. I will bring my son and then they will meet each other.'

In the meantime I saw more photos of Iqbal and he saw mine. I liked his photos very much! I thought, 'Yes he is handsome!' I believed he was very good looking and later he said he liked my photo too, so that was good. We finally met in 1978 in London, when my father and I landed at Heathrow Airport. I was very happy, but very nervous. He looked nice, but looks are not everything. He was nervous too, I could tell, when we met. We went to a restaurant and had coffee and cake. I remember it was a self-service place. You went to the counter and got your food, and we had lots to eat. I think we were both anxious about the first meeting. But it went very well. It was very good between us right from that day. Later Iqbal and his father went back to Manchester and we stayed in London. Then after twenty or twenty-five days we got married!

An arranged marriage could not have worked better for me. I was very happy to marry Iqbal. I knew I would come to love him. We are the same age, which is good. I had been studying in Bangladesh for my A-levels at that time. I finished my

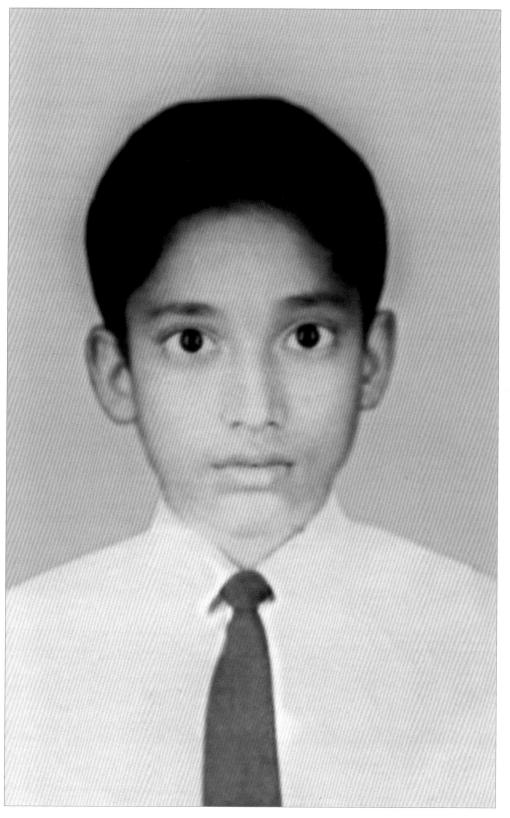

1969 – aged thirteen.

Above: 1986 – Grandmother and my cousin Shahnoor in the garden of the house in Sylhet.

Below left: A photo of me aged twenty, taken in 1976 . . .

Below right: . . . and a more formal one taken two years later.

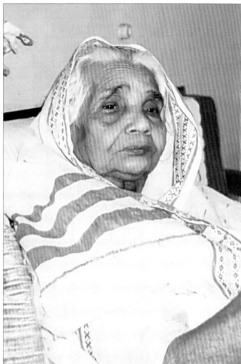

Above left: 1987 – My father, Al Hajj Abdul Khalis.

Above right: My grandmother, Syeda Afrozun Nessa.

Below: 1986 – with Salma, my wife, at the Taj Mahal.

Above: 2004 – in Venice with my oldest daughter, Shahida.

Below: 1993 – the opening of the first Seamark factory in Openshaw, Manchester, with John Selwyn Gummer (now Lord Deben), the then Minister for Agriculture, Fisheries and Food.

Above: 1988 – donating a cheque for flood victims in Bangladesh.

Below: 1995 – with the Prince of Wales at the IFE at Earls Court in London.

Above: 2000 – the official opening of the Seamark factory in Bangladesh with HRH The Princess Royal.

Below: 1992 – outside the Red Fort restaurant in London's Soho with Emma Thompson, John Snow and Glenys Kinnock (Baroness Kinnock of Holyhead).

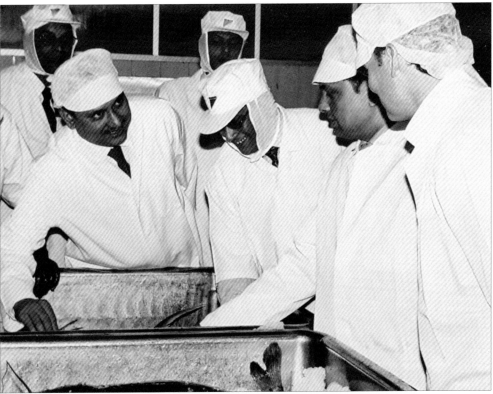

Above: With my siblings in 2003: (from left to right) Jusna, Kamal, Rahela, Shajna, Bilal, me.

Below: 2004 – Anwar Choudhury, the then British High Commissioner (second from right) visits the Seamark factory in Bangladesh.

2001 – outside Buckingham Palace with my wife, Salma, after the investiture for my OBE.

exams, then I came here. It was a huge thing to be brought to Great Britain to meet a new man who was to be my husband. My mother-in-law and father-in-law, as well as my husband's brothers and sister, already lived in Oldham, so I was joining a big family. They all made me very welcome.

In my family I had two sisters and one brother. I was the eldest child of our family and Iqbal was eldest in his. I think this was another factor that drew us together. We were definitely not pushed into this marriage. Both our parents advised us to take time to get to know each other, but I think we knew from the very first time we met that we wanted to be together. We were very happy and neither of us had any doubts then or since that we were doing the right thing. We started a new life in Oldham and then after one year Iqbal's parents went back to Bangladesh.

Iqbal was the first man my parents ever suggested I marry. It had never happened before. I had never had any other husbands suggested to me. When I was eighteen, I kept hearing my mother and father talking about my possible future husband. I knew they were talking about Iqbal and my husband later told me that it was the same for him. He had heard my name mentioned before we met. Our parents were right, we were very good for each other, and we still are. Both lots of parents tried very hard to find someone suitable and until my father-in-law died he remained a good friend of my father.

I have seen lots of pictures of my father and Iqbal's father together. They seemed to meet up every weekend; they were so close. It was fortunate that my father came over to this country to study otherwise perhaps my husband and I would never have met. When we met at Heathrow and I first saw him, I thought, 'Yeah!' When I first saw his picture I liked the look of him and when I saw him in real life he was just the same. He was a handsome young man – and he still is handsome!!!

It was a huge thing for a young girl, but I felt good about it from the start. It was not as if I was meeting someone from some strange family. The first time I was in the country, everything was new, then a month after meeting at Heathrow we were married in a nice restaurant. It was very exciting; we talked a lot on the telephone in the time up to the wedding.

We were very happy together right from the start. The system of arranged marriages worked well but in our day things were different. In our day you met, you talked and if you were happy with your chosen partner then you got married. It worked very well for us, but nowadays I think young people tend to want to make their own choices.

Before the Heathrow meeting it was building up in my mind all the time, I had seen photos and I liked the look of this man. We met after two years, during which time there had been so much talking, talking, talking, a long time. I was studying and I said to him, 'I will finish my exams then I will come.'

When we met, very soon I thought, 'Oh yes I like him!' I was very happy. If I had not liked him I could have pulled out of it. My family would never have forced me to marry someone I did not want to marry. I think our system is a good way of choosing a partner. It worked very well for us. If you want to do anything good you have to be patient. Iqbal is a very strong character, he always talked about his dreams of working hard and making money. He was always very keen to get on in life, even when he was young. He wanted to do this and he wanted to do that. He convinced me he was going to really make something of himself.

I felt so lucky to be married to a man who felt like such a

good husband. He was very dynamic and ambitious, and hard-working. Also he had a very good sense of humour, which is very important. We were thinking about children quite soon and they started to come along after we had been married for nearly two years.

But before then, after we were married in London, we went back to Oldham. The family home was a small terraced house. But at that time they had two houses next door that were knocked together inside. It was a shop as well. There was lots of room. It had five bedrooms, I believe, and there was a sitting room at the top. England was grey and cold after Bangladesh, both in London and Oldham. We got married in May and even though it was coming into summer, it felt cold to me. It was cloudy and cold mostly, but the day we got married it was so sunny. I was so happy.

After one year we all went back, us and his parents, to Bangladesh to see our family and friends. We stayed for two months and then I came back with my husband. My family did not come back with us. They just came once a year for two or three week holiday. Iqbal's mother was a very strong personality, but I got on very well with her. She was always kind and thoughtful towards me.

Iqbal has always been very charismatic and I was very pleased to become his wife. I believe if you love someone where he takes you to live doesn't matter. A small house? Under a tree? It doesn't matter, if it's true love. Now we have a lovely house, but I didn't mind cold Oldham and a terraced house. I was just very happy for us to be together.

The shop was open, but I did not work in the shop. Kamal and my husband and Bilal after he came back from school, did that. I didn't get involved in the business because I knew he wouldn't want his wife working in the shop with him. My husband always wanted to build a bigger business. He was not content to work in the shop. He has always been the same, wanting to build bigger and better. He always drives on, wanting to be more and more successful and build a better business. He has so much energy and he does so much thinking, good thinking! And he has lots of ambition. I liked that in him when I first met him, and he has not changed; he is still very ambitious.

Iqbal used to wake up very early to start work when he was young; now he is not so young he still wakes up early. He used to get up at six o'clock in the morning – now it is seven o'clock – to go to the markets where he would buy, buy, buy. Now he is still buying.

At first Iqbal was very busy delivering to all customers. First he would be on the telephone getting the orders then they would do the deliveries. He had to visit many people. Kamal and Bilal joined him later. They bought a warehouse and soon after they built a cold storage. I was involved with the children more, he was out a lot, but we always came together at dinner once a day. That was very important to him and important to all of us, the whole family. He always came home by eight o'clock whenever possible so we could have good family time together. He was always keen to look after the children and made sure they got good tuition. He was always very determined that they had a good education. When he comes home at eight o'clock from work that is the end of his business day, there is no more work, family is very important to him,

Iqbal was very impressive as a young man. He has always been impressive to me. He goes to bed always at half past eleven. When he goes to bed, in five minutes he is asleep. He sleeps well because, he says, 'I didn't do anything bad. I didn't do anything wrong. If people do bad things maybe they can't sleep, but I sleep very well always because as soon as my eyes close in bed I am asleep.'

I did not experience any racial problems when I arrived and began to live in Oldham, I did not feel uncomfortable, but I did not go out to work. I went out to meet friends and I went out to university as I continued studying. At that time we were encouraged to learn English. When I arrived at Heathrow I didn't know enough English to speak to Iqbal. We first spoke in Bengali, or Bangla. We still speak Bangla to each other. It is our first language and our children do too. Bangladesh has changed a lot. Today it has high society and low society, and some very rich people and great contrasts. In England people seem more similar.

Iqbal is used to women with strong character like my mother-in-law, who was also a very clever lady. I am very soft, gentle person who is not very strong, but my husband does listen to me. Iqbal is very much the head of our family. My mother-in-law says as he is the oldest brother, you have to listen to what he says, right or wrong. I think he is pretty well right all the time! He taught both of his brothers all about the business and they do as he says; they accept he is leader and they follow.

I am happy not to be involved in the business. Maybe if I had done so from beginning then that would have been different. But now it is so big I don't want to get involved. He likes to have separate home from work, he does not bring work home too much, that works for us.

In fact, we could have met when we were teenagers. I was

in Sylhet at the same time as my husband, but I didn't know him and nor did our family know his family then.

I remember in 1971, I was in Sylhet then as a schoolgirl because my father was in England at that time. My grandfather and grandmother came to Sylhet so I studied there. When the Liberation War was being fought we struggled quite a lot. I didn't see any fighting, but we were always on the move running, running, running. When warplanes came above we hid in a huge underpass behind the garden or when the sirens sounded in the town that meant everybody should go out of the house and into a huge shelter. We would rush into that, just leave food or whatever and go.

Iqbal is still the man I married. He hasn't changed much over the years. He still works hard all the time and he is still driven. But he always makes lots of time for holidays even though he still works hard. He is romantic – he still gives me flowers. He is still young.

And we still laugh a lot together. Now we can laugh at some of the disasters of the early years. Sometimes he was let down by a supplier and the fish was not good. And when he flew mangoes in from Pakistan I remember the house was full of mangoes. It was terrible, we had so many and nowhere to put them. . .

CHAPTER ELEVEN

BACK TO IQBAL

Marriage was wonderful. Salma came into my life and brightened it from the start. It was a huge responsibility for me, but up to the time I got married I was not enjoying life at all. It was always work, work, work. And this is where my wife made a huge contribution. We loved each other and we trusted each other right from the start. She made a huge contribution to everything because she entered the marriage so wholeheartedly. She had not a single doubt that we were right for each other and happily, I felt exactly the same way. We were both very lucky.

Salma is a very mature person and whatever subject I share with she gives good advice. At first I was working away a great deal. I hardly took her out. That was the greatness of her: she accepted that I was very busy building up the business. She could have dragged me out of the family and said, 'Why are you taking care of everyone? We should enjoy our own lives.' But she is so warm and generous, she would not think of saying that. I will always be grateful to her for her support, particularly in those difficult early years. I think she is beautiful in heart and she loved me and the whole family. My grandmother and my father made a really good choice.

My grandmother used to say, 'She is your wife but I have chosen her! Don't forget.'

CHAPTER TWELVE

STARTING BUSINESS

As I settled down to enjoy life as a married man I was more determined than ever to make the business bigger and better. Now that I had finally decided to come back to Oldham for good there were no doubts in my mind. Even as a young man I was always very positive. If you don't believe in yourself then how can you expect anyone else to? That was my philosophy and it still is.

I have always considered appearance to be very important. It is the way you are first judged, before anyone has heard a word you have to say. An attractive appearance creates a good first impression. So I always took great care of how I looked. I was not vain; I was just being professional! I used to make sure I was always well dressed, and well groomed, and I knew I was good looking. I was nearly 6ft tall – well, 5ft 10 and half an inch! I never forget the half an inch! I had fashionably long hair and I always made sure I was nicely spoken. I hope it does not sound too vain, but the girls used to look at me, especially in the North.

There was a huge difference between London and Oldham, and even London and Manchester, in those days. As soon as I arrived in London I could see that most people were far more stylishly dressed than they were in Manchester. Now I don't think it is so marked. The same branded shops are everywhere. They all have the same shirts, the same suits and the same shoes. In old days it was not like that. When I used to go to London I wore flared trousers, platform shoes, a long white scarf, a leather jacket and a maxi coat. Luckily I had friends who owned a leather-garment factory so I did not have to pay for my leather jacket. As soon as I came back to Manchester Piccadilly train station, I felt all the girls and boys were looking at me. I could see them thinking, 'He looks different.' So as you can imagine, I had a lot of respect from my father and the family. I know they were proud of me.

I managed to raise a bit of capital, as I've already explained, from my father's friends and it was enough to buy a vehicle. My first Transit van was pretty old but it was all I could afford. It cost £335 of the money I had borrowed, which I had to pay up front. I was paying them back in instalments, as much as I could afford. The van was white of course. Every vehicle I bought was white because that colour reflects the heat best and keeps the contents inside cooler. To start with, my friend Khurshed Alam did a lot of the driving because I couldn't drive. At least he had a licence, which was more than I had!

As well as giving me driving lessons, Khurshed gave me a lot of good advice over the years, he used to talk to me about everything. He was wise and quite inspirational. He had previously run businesses but when I knew him he was semi-retired. He was quite old and he had become a driving instructor; he also had a property business. He guided me, showed me where to make a good deal and where to buy things. He let me in on some of the business tricks that you learn in your early days.

We used to go to the wholesale markets together to buy our produce. Most often we went to Smithfield market in Manchester. The first time I went to Smithfield and put my hand up to bid I found it very difficult. I can remember it well; I was with Khurshed Alam. But while it was difficult, it was also very enjoyable.

When I saw the big merchants, with so many products, it made me wish I was in business like them. I could make so much more money than with this little shop, I thought. I wanted to be supplying all the shops, not just running one. My father had laid the foundations with his shop; all I had to do was add to it. I took a lot of risks, but there are many good things about Bangladeshi people and one of them is that if you go to them and ask for help, and you have a good reputation, they will help you.

Soon I was supplying many of the shops and all of the restaurants in Manchester. I had a few senior friends who helped me. When I started talking to them I explained that this was what I wanted to do, to supply people. Even in those days I had a vision that one day I would import goods and sell them on. There were so many things at that time were not available in this country.

In no time at all, within less than five years, I would become bigger than many of the shops and restarants I supplied. Within five years I would go and sell to them. At first we just bought produce for our shop, but quite soon we started to buy for neighbouring shops and then for shops a little further away. The expansion was very swift. This first stage of business all happened in within six months. We knocked on many, many doors to get more customers and supplied more and more shops. I worked very, very hard, but I never minded that. I learned early on in business that you have to seize your moment. Once the window of opportunity opens for you, it is essential to galvanise your efforts and take advantage or the chance could be lost.

I talked to lots of people and I worked hard to learn the business of being a wholesaler. Fortunately, I had a few friends who were already wholesalers, and I bought stock and started selling to the restaurants in the area. My father was pleased to see that I was throwing myself into working hard. I suppose I was lucky that I was able to borrow a bit of money, but as I said, good Bangladeshi people will always help each other, especially in a foreign land.

It might sound easy now, looking back many years later, but it was anything but easy at the time; it was a big challenge. This was after I got married in 1978. My wife was so supportive. I could never have managed to achieve it if I had not had her to care for me. She was wonderful; she still is! The pace of change took us both a little by surprise. It seemed like it happened very quickly, but I always had a plan prepared in advance. I was always pushing to get more customers, to increase the range and volume of products. When you have a plan you just go and do it; you don't think or worry that it won't work because you have your advance plan. I started with money borrowed from family friends and of course I paid it back straightaway.

Khurshed is one of the many people who helped me. I have a long list of people I am grateful to for their assistance. I will never forget them. Being in business felt good, even in the early days when I was just finding my way. I enjoyed the feeling of working for myself. When I get involved in something I want to get ahead, and go on and on, and succeed. I never get sick and tired of work. I want to get the job done. I struggled sometimes, but at the same time I wanted to expand as soon as I started. Once I had my old Transit, I wanted to buy a bigger new van as soon as I'd made enough money. I knew I was in a good place for making money. There was a shortage of suppliers so there were opportunities. It wasn't always easy; sometimes the restaurants didn't buy enough, but they never rejected us.

Of course it was very basic and hand to mouth in those early days. I bought all sorts of foodstuffs the restaurants needed. At Smithfield Market I soon made a few friends and bought lots of different produce, all the things restaurants require. You name it, I bought it! I used to go to the restaurants and take a list and then just buy whatever they needed and supply them. At the start, in order to set it up, I was knocking on doors. But often I knew the owners. Some of them were my father's friends. Strangely, sometimes I was considered superior because I'd lived in London! It meant I could talk with more confidence and conviction. It felt like, 'I'm from the capital and I'm talking to people from the village.' They really liked the idea that I was their countryman and yet I had experience in one of the biggest cities in the world. London was regarded with great awe by many of our people, particularly those who had hardly ever spent any time there. I had no fear of talking to anyone. I said with great confidence,

'I want to do business and you are my customer and you have to support me. I can supply you with whatever you want to buy.' That's how I started.

But obviously there were difficulties. Some people I was competing with were not too happy about my arrival on the scene. There was always an existing supplier and they were always really furious with me. But they were not smart like me. I have always been smart in my dealings.

The business was very difficult at times, but I never give up. I sold to restaurants and shops in Oldham and Manchester. I knocked on a lot of doors and had to face a lot of rejection among my successes. It was not an easy business because it was very competitive and sometimes it was hard to get the money. A friend, who used to supply poultry, advised me: 'You have to go in when a restaurant is very busy. You have to go in and ask for payment of your invoice and stand at the counter when there are a lot of customers around. Then they will give you your money.' It was a trick, he told me. I'd asked him how was that he'd get paid and I didn't and he said, 'Eight o'clock is the best time, when the restaurant is full!'

There was a market in Bradford where lot of Asian people from the big concentration of immigrants in the city worked and visited. I made some good friends there and they helped me to source products. They helped me with information on which Asian vegetables to supply. I also learned a lot about shrimps, prawns, fish, you name it. I wanted to know everything there was to know about all household and catering requirements.

I acquired an immense amount of valuable knowledge from the suppliers. Many of them became my friends. They helped me and I helped them. It worked both ways. They wanted to sell stuff and so did I. They were a very decent kind of people and there was a huge and growing demand for supplying good food to the restaurants. I had found a new niche market.

After buying the Ford Transit, the next big step was to install a small cold storage unit inside the shop in Oldham. Jimmy Lorentz, and his brothers John and Rob, from St Helens, built that one and they've built all our cold storage ever since. Later we bought our first big Mercedes van. At first we could not afford to have a proper freezer van. The early ones were insulated, which meant we could keep food frozen for a few hours. We often had to move quickly, although in winter we didn't need it! We ran it for about two years like this, and then we saw huge opportunities for expansion.

I moved on. I started to import vegetables and fruits such as mangoes. After getting married, my wife and I visited Bangladesh and I met up with my childhood friend Shahid from Dhaka. After the Liberation War he and his family moved to Pakistan where they originally came from. We met and he told me people were exporting mangoes to the Middle East. 'How about in England?' he said. 'Will you be able to import them?' Of course, that's just what I did. Everything that was a possible niche business I grabbed. We were to introduce mangoes to the UK, one of the first families to import mangoes from Pakistan.

Shahid and I have done business for a long time. I have moved forward at every stage of the business. I started supplying the restaurants, then the grocery shops and the supermarkets. Then I thought now I want to import, in bulk, in huge quantities. I always wanted to import.

After the mangoes, I thought about how about importing fish too. When Bangladeshi, Indian and Pakistani families came to the UK I knew they would want fish, so I started importing it from Bangladesh, Pakistan, Thailand, India and Kenya. It was a big operation. At that time Bangladeshi restaurants were growing everywhere like mushrooms. Restaurants make a massive contribution to the economy. In the late 1960s and early 1970s not many liked curries, but tastes gradually changed and curry and other good Asian dishes became more popular. When men used to get drunk in the UK, they would go for a curry. Chicken tikka masala and vindaloo became national dishes. The curry industry grew and now people are addicted.

We started to import a lot of products by air and later by ship. We imported container loads of seafood products like prawns, shrimps and dry products such as spices. Slowly I became more ambitious; I wanted to start a processing plant. In those days there were many fishing companies in existence. We used to import semi-processed shrimps from all over the world and they used to do all the cooking and value adding, and I wanted to do this myself. And then I wanted to do the exporting. So I put up my first purposely built shrimp-processing factory in 1991 in Openshaw, Manchester. The building, housing one of the largest cold-storage facilities in the North-West in those days, as well as the processing factory and offices, was officially opened by John Gummer in 1993, when he was the Minister of Agriculture, Fisheries and Food. The following year, Tony Baldry MP inaugurated our most advanced cooking and IQF (individually quick frozen) shrimps production facility for consumer packs.

Before that we started distributing and then we built a lot of warehouses, a lot of depots. We wanted to be able to distribute everywhere in UK. Then we set up the factory, which had a huge production capacity, In addition to machinery from the UK, I also imported machinery from Denmark and Germany, all food-graded stainless steel. To me it was like a brand new factory when it opened. The place was like a nuclear power plant, everywhere shining steel and everyone wearing white high-visibility outfits. They looked very smart and were trained very well by the Danish food-processing company Carnitech.

Then I become ambitious. I remember there was a Manchester Chamber of Commerce seminar to promote export business to small and medium companies in the North-West, hosted by Business Link and supported by the DTI. We were an active member of the chamber so I went to it and there was the then British High Commissioner to Bangladesh, Peter Fowler. I happened to be sitting next to him when the presenter was talking about the Queen's Award for Export Achievement. I became interested. I thought, 'This sounds OK. How do you get it?' I asked a lot of questions about the volume of exports and how the award was decided, and it was explained to me that if you had managed to have continuous growth in exports you could apply. That information never left my mind and I knew I had a very good chance of achieving it. I applied, and in 1998 we received the Queen's Award for our export performance. By that time we exported all over Europe and USA.

But as usual I'm getting way ahead of myself. . . My brother Kamal joined in the business when I started making a success of the wholesale business. He is four years younger than me and he joined about five years after I started. Then Bilal, my other brother, the baby in the family, is eight years younger and he joined quite late. We created divisions. I was more on the administrative side and looking after the finances. Kamal was very good at the factories and export responsibilities, which he still controls, and Bilal took over the national account and all the ethnic business, including major supermarkets. Family is strength. Both Kamal and Bilal were the most influential men in the business. Without them I could not have done it all. It was the family effort that brought success. They worked very hard and they still do. I am very grateful, they are brothers, they are friends and they are partners. We never had any arguments; we trust each other implicitly.

Kamal Ahmed thanks his older brother for everything: 'Iqbal is remarkable. His energy and his insight have driven our success from the day he started. I am proud to have him as my leader and I trust him implicitly. His mind is so fast and far-seeing he has directed the business brilliantly.'

Bilal Ahmed agrees wholeheartedly: 'I feel very lucky to have Iqbal as my older brother. It is traditional with us that the older brother is the leader and when the older brother is Iqbal there is no question this is the best policy. His energy and his foresight and his business sense are superb. I am delighted to have him as a leader and as a brother.'

That is kind of my brothers, but also on my part, it is great to have them with me in the business. It is so wonderful for me to share the success of Seamark with the whole family. Our father and mother saw much of the early development and they were so proud to see the family doing well together.

If I can go back in time for a moment, to when I started wholesaling. My father wasn't well, and he decided to go back to Bangladesh to live. He decided that England was not the country he wanted to live in. We still had the big house in the village and the land and estates and the house in the city of Sylhet. I think he left in 1981, three years after I got married. He and my mother both left. I was sad but I understood.

My father stayed in Bangladesh and enjoyed his life there. I go back to Bangladesh a great deal because I have a lot of businesses there.

CHAPTER THIRTEEN

GETTING DISCRIMINATION OFF MY CHEST

I t wasn't that easy. If I am honest, and I am determined to be, every step of my life was difficult. It is only in the last ten or fifteen years that it has become much easier, since I received recognition with the Queen's Award for export achievement and the OBE for services to international trade, and when I became involved with many government advisory boards. Now I not only speak for myself but for my community.

Until these recent years, I was discriminated against. There is no doubt about that. In the earlier days, when we wanted to build a factory, it wasn't easy. It was very difficult. We couldn't buy land to build a factory. I believe this was probably because we came from Bangladesh. The local authorities did not seem to believe that I would be capable of building a good building. I approached the city council in the early 1990s wanting to build the best factory in Manchester. It was before the recession and things were really moving after the end of

Margaret Thatcher's era. The local authority said, 'No, no, no. We are not allowing you to build a factory on the main road. We want a nice glass car showroom on that site.' I pleaded that I was going to create a great development there, bringing hundreds of jobs to an area desperately short of employment. But the local authorities said no. That site is still vacant! I am talking about twenty-five years later now. Then I proposed a large development in Parkhouse Street and my scheme was created by top architects and professional structural engineers. And they said, 'The colour scheme is not right!' or 'The size of the building is not right!' It was nitpicking, which I believe was inspired by the colour of my skin. We spent so much money to create a brilliant scheme, but time and time again we were rejected. We could guess what was happening. You can buy a garage if you are not from my part of the world. But you can't build a factory.

CHAPTER FOURTEEN

BACK TO THE BEGINNING

As soon as I started supplying restaurants with goods, I really threw myself into it heart and soul. Fortunately, I am a very quick learner. When I started I really hit the ground running. You see, I have always been able to learn different things very quickly. I catch up on everything – learning the ways of a new country, languages, friends!

Getting the business started was something in my life that also happened very fast. The platform was there. My father had set it up. The business was started. I just changed direction as soon as I got into the driving seat. Another very interesting thing is that I have so much belief in my own ability that I would never, ever work for anybody else. I didn't want a job, I wanted to build a business. I wanted to do something different. This is what influenced my father to help me, I think, and everybody in the family to also help me. My father created a good starting point and asked his friends to help me, and they certainly did as he asked. For example, if I wanted to deliver to a particular restaurant he would ring the owner and explain about my business and they would take goods from me.

Those early introductions were very, very valuable. It was fantastic and he was fantastic.. There were many moments, from 1978 onwards, when it was as if a bell rang in my brain and I thought I had the right idea. This was also a time of massive numbers of Bangladeshis arriving in Great Britain of Bangladeshi. Thousands of them started bringing their family. This was partly because there were huge food shortages in Bangladesh at this time as well as enormous political problems.

Earlier it used to be the case that people came to England expecting to earn some money for a while and then go back home. But the people who left Bangladesh during such tough times were different. They were not going to go back and who can blame them. I think everybody in the UK realised that it was not worth going back to an ailing Bangladesh when Britain was doing so well. In 1979 Margaret Thatcher came in and introduced privatisation of lots of services. People were working hard in general; they had jobs and were more comfortable and by that time, equal opportunities were starting to improve. Lots of telephone calls were made home describing how it was to live in the relative comfort of Great Britain. And when people in Great Britain who talked to their family in Bangladesh told them about the standard of living in their new homes the folks back home were impressed.

I could see the potential for my business. In just three years almost everybody who arrived from Bangladesh was bringing their family over. I realised that in ten years' time there would be thousands of restaurants and I thought, 'Oh My God we'll need more and more produce to supply the restaurants to feed them all.' In those days it seemed that anyone opening a restaurant just couldn't go wrong. I could see that there would not only be more restaurants opening but also more grocery shops, more cafés and much more household consumption.

I realised there would be a massive increase in the need for food. We started importing natural sweet-water fish from the mighty rivers of Meghna and Jamuna. There weren't many fish farms back then, just natural fish cultivation. As consumption was swiftly increasing in the early eighties, we started to import fish and other products from Thailand. At that time Thailand was a country booming with tourism and agriculture, like China was ten years ago. I sent my brother Kamal there first to check out the potential and later I went myself to Thailand to see if we could source some products. At that time I was getting food from Pakistan and freshwater fish from Canada. We started importing freshwater carp and all sorts of other kind of fish just to feed our Bangladeshi community and otherss as well.

When I travelled to Thailand I saw the fish was very good value, so I started buying a lot. There was great produce of all kinds. We found it to be a great source of fish and also vegetables and I think we imported from Thailand for nearly twenty years. We made a fortune out of it, the shrimp and fish industries were very good for us.

CHAPTER FIFTEEN

FAMILY

When I got married I already had my own car. My father bought me a Mark III Ford Cortina. I've still got a picture of it. It made such a fantastic difference to our lives. Every weekend my wife and I used to go out in that car. We would drive off to take the family to Southport or Blackpool, or the Lake District. There are so many beautiful places to visit. My wife really liked England straight away and it was great to be able to show her all these places. We enjoyed travelling all over the country. I worked hard but I always made time for my family, for my wife, for my mother, for all the members of my family. We loved to have parties and my house has always been open for my family – we always have great get-togethers! I love to invite my friends round, too. We cooked some great barbecues, had many picnics and they produced a lot of happy memories.

The business started just before the marriage. I knew there

was a future in what I was doing in both areas! In my life I think that every decision I made was well calculated, the timing absolutely right. I always make sure that I think ahead, in terms of business and in terms of family. I plan pretty well everything. For example, when our three children came along I wanted to give them the best possible education; they all went to good schools. I knew that was a good investment. It wasn't easy to find the money sometimes, but what can be more important than investing in your children's future?

My children are all bright but my older daughter was brilliant. They all went to the private nursery, one of the best in the area. It was very expensive. When it was time for my older daughter to go to secondary school I wanted her to go to the grammar school in Oldham, Hulme Grammar School. It is famous but in those days hardly any coloured people attended those schools. All the pupils seemed to be white. I wanted to get my daughter into that school but it was difficult.

I didn't know what to do. Then I remembered that my friendly bank manager at the time, Alec Dodgeon, came from Saddleworth in Oldham. I went to see him and said, 'Alec, I would like you to help me. You are from Oldham and I hope you know somebody at the school. I am having difficulty getting my daughter in and she is brilliant, you know. I am happy to pay the tuition fees.'

'Leave it to me,' he said and he found out that one of the maths teachers at the school was an old school friend of his. He spoke to the teacher, who asked me to take my daughter there to see him, and after that visit they eventually took her. I had another, much longer, relationship with Alec Dodgeon, which I will talk about later. He was a very important man in my life.

There was a lady used to come to our shop and when I told her my problems she said was a school inspector. I told her that I wanted my daughter to attend the grammar school. 'Oh it's going to cost you,' she said. So even after Alec had set up the appointment I was very careful to keep an eye on things.

When I attended the appointment, the people at the school told me several times that this would be 'very expensive' for my daughter. We would have to buy the specified uniform from Kendals, the store in Deansgate, Manchester. In those days there were very few good shops. I said, 'I don't mind.' Then they spelled out the school fees and so on and I said, 'Yes.' I think they wanted to check whether I knew these things and if I knew how to conduct myself. Fortunately, there was no racism in the school. My children did not experience any problems.

My daughter went to the school and enjoyed it very much and then I put my son into that school followed by my younger daughter and my nephew and my niece. Most of our children went to Hulme Grammar School and they all did very well. They were clever and with the excellent teaching the results were very good. My daughter was always number one or two in her class, good at all the sciences and she says my daughter says that was the best years she had. A lot of girls from the school later became doctors.

I loved going to the school. That is one thing I never missed, my children's parents' evenings. My wife and I went to every single one. No matter where I travelled, I always felt I had to be there and I always made sure I talked to the teachers and that my children were receiving good attention. 'Where do they sit? Do they respond in class?' I asked. And lots more questions. Sometimes my daughter used to get upset and say,

'Papa, why do you have to go and ask all those questions?' I replied, 'Look I'm paying for it. I am entitled to ask.'

I would say that probably any immigrant, anyone who comes from a background like mine, always fears going back to that situation. That is why I always want to be pushing on. I always take care that my children and my family don't get that kind of treatment I suffered. I don't think they experienced racism or discrimination. They don't believe in it. That generation does not have the same thoughts as mine did. I think things have improved greatly from my time, but that would not have been difficult.

Here's another interesting story! Being in the seafood business we are also in the fish business. Selling fish is not a good profession in Bangladeshi culture. It's something that quite low caste people normally do. It is different here, where selling fish is quite respectable. Before I built a factory, I wanted to set up a fish farm because I enjoy fishing. Business brings out creative ideas in me. I had 600 acres of land offered to me by the government of Bangladesh, which I accepted and put a name to: National Fish Culture. As soon as the sign went up, my mother says, 'What is this?' There is a picture of the fish. She is not impressed by my very public link-up with the fish business.

'Look, Mum, don't get upset. I've not become a fish stall man. I have opened a business about fish cultivation. I will take it, process it and sell it to England,' I said.

'But what is the board on our house,' she asked.

'Oh, this is just the office, we will make an office upstairs in one room.'

'No, no, no, it is not a good idea, Iqbal.' I asked why. 'In this country, selling fish is not a good profession and people

114

look at us. You have two sisters we need to find husbands for. The fish business is not going to help them at all. Your sisters at home will not find husbands because of the fish business. So it is not a good idea.'

So I said to the workman, 'Hey, hang on, don't put the board up!' because I respected my mother and her judgment. That is the truth. I knew the feeling about fish sellers, but to be honest I had not thought it through properly. My mother was right, of course.

I had to accept the culture we have in Bangladesh of always respecting your mother. She did not want people coming up to me in the street and saying, 'Oh you have become a fisherman now!' I took the board down – but that did not stop me selling fish. I have fishing trawlers in the Bay of Bengal catching fish twenty-four hours a day, processing them at sea onboard!

Regardless of your background or your training or where you come from, what is important is your vision and, with all your efforts, how successful you can become. If you are catching fish and selling it so you can feed your family, I think that is quite a good profession. If you can farm the fish and export the fish then you can provide work for thousands of people, so being a fisherman can be a very good profession indeed. Not forgetting, of course, that eating fish is good for you!

CHAPTER SIXTEEN

PRAWNS

Whatever I do I want to be the best. As soon as I became established as a wholesaler I wanted to be the best wholesaler of them all. So I was always seeking to widen my range and bring in top-quality products. Quite soon my thoughts turned to king prawns. We love king prawns in our country and I knew British people would feel the same. I realised this tastiest of seafood could be really popular in my new home country. So I set about trying to import king prawns.

I was convinced king prawns could become really popular and I desperately wanted to import them. It wasn't so easy. I went to Bangladesh to find suppliers, but I couldn't find anybody to do the job. Then when I continued the search in London I was delighted to make contact with a man from my own country who said he could provide me with what I wanted. It was simple, and perhaps a little too good to be true. 'I want to buy prawns,' I said. He said, 'Yes I will do it.' He seemed very genuine and after negotiating for one or two days with him we agreed a deal. He asked for a deposit of £50,000 by telegraphic transfer into his account. I was so innocent in those days. Remember, this was very early in my business career, but it did not take me very long to realise that this was a very bad move.

The next thing I know this guy has disappeared and so has my £50,000. I telephoned and somebody answered and said, 'Wrong number.' There was no trace of him. Three months went by and four months, I was getting desperate for my money. This was far more than I could afford to lose and I didn't know what to do. Then I talked to one of my relatives who held a very powerful position in Bangladesh, a lieutenant colonel in the army. I was in touch with him and I explained that this guy took my money and never sent a shipment. My relative promised he would help me if he could.

Very happily for me my army-officer relative was as good as his word; the military was in power at the time. He found the guy who owed me the money and sent some soldiers round accusing the man of being a thief. They said: 'You took money from my relative and you don't respond. Why?' My cheating supplier knew then that he was in big trouble. In no time at all he sent me a shipment and called me, saying, 'Please help me, the soldiers are going to shoot me.' He was terrified. I made a lot of money dealing with him. There is nothing like having an army on your side!

Then I started getting ambitious! I wanted to buy much larger quantities of king prawns and import them. By air you could only get one ton or two tons at a time and it was not good enough. I started searching for a way to transport them by ship, something that had not been done before.

PRAWNS

I wanted to bring frozen prawns over on a ship in quantities of 30 or 40 tons. I always think big! I went to Bangladesh and I found somebody who could ship me that sort of quantity, so I booked a consignment. These were the days before the giant refrigerated containers dominated world trade. But Bangladesh's own shipping line had a ship with a cold-storage unit inside. They insisted that they could ship frozen product to the UK. I talked to the shipping line and found out that the ship with the cold-storage unit was coming to Dundee with jute. This was in the early 1980s and $46,000 dollars was the price I paid. The ship's journey was long and slow, but it eventually arrived in Scotland after three months at sea.

The forwarding agency was Patterson, who handled the jute. We gave them the documents to release our consignment. I knew it was a huge risk and sure enough when we received the consignment it was $7,500 worth of shrimps short! What do you do? I think we made a big profit anyway, so it was not the end of the world. Yet I wanted to know who had stolen this huge portion of king prawns. I think we made a claim against the insurers that was accepted and we recovered the loss. Patterson investigated what had happened and it turned out that the prawns were not stolen by pirates and the ship was not short loaded. Instead, of all things, the missing prawns were eaten by the crew! They had obviously fancied a more interesting diet on their long voyage, so who were the insurers going to sue or claim from?

James Finlay, the shipping company, inspected the consignment according to our letter of credit, so we couldn't put a claim against them. Hundreds of crew could have been involved, so who are you going to claim against? The man who shipped the goods became even more interested in exporting to Great Britain with me. He kept chasing me to send more. I said, 'I will not be taking the Bangladesh shipping line any more. Sorry.' Instead I went to Singapore, because at that time I was importing from Malaysia and Indonesia. There was quite a time gap until finally I met a guy and told my story. He said, 'Why don't you buy from Bangladesh? I can get in touch with the Maersk shipping line.

I talked to Maersk and it was hopeful but complicated. They said, 'We can't talk to you because we have an agent in Bangladesh.' But that agent only handled dry containers. I was told I needed a quay on the port to plug in my container to an electrical outlet. The Maersk boss said he could arrange for their agent to meet me next time I visited. So on my next trip I went and stayed in same hotel as the agent. We talked and he said, 'If you can guarantee to use fifty containers a year, we can give you some containers.' They had to come loaded; if they came empty they would lose money. Without the fifty containers they could not create all the necessary infrastructure and plug-in system. I had no idea whether I could do fifty containers. I just didn't know, but nevertheless I said, 'Yes' and signed. It was a kind of bluff. The owner of Maersk was Mr A P Muller. He inaugurated the reefer (refrigerated) containers in Chittagong and invited me along to the opening, but I didn't go in case I could not fulfil what I'd signed for, but within six months, I had used fifty containers. That was in 1984 and I made a lot of money. Maersk was at that time a small shipping line, but it has grown and is now everywhere. The speed at which it grew is amazing.

My brother Kamal got involved and helped with deliveries,

but by then our original cold room in Oldham was too small for us. The next-door neighbour was complaining that building a cold room might make his house cold! I laughed and explained that the insulation panels seal and prevent the cold moving outwards. He still called the local environment people and they caused a few problems. Eventually they came and said everything was OK. I made sure the neighbour was happy and satisfied.

Business was good. We were getting more containers by sea, and we still had vegetables brought in by air. When we built a cold room next to the shop we were still buying by air as well as importing container loads. But it was not easy to unload a container in front of the shop because they were such huge things. So we found a local cold-storage facility and unloaded there instead. We used to keep all the products inside the public cold storage, then every two days bring them back to our cold storage; from there we used to distribute. It was a lot of hard work. Of course I used to help the boys unloading the containers as well as supervising and directing them. It was four or five years of very hard physical work as well as the mental work involved in building the business. I was gradually increasing the number of people we employed and the quantity of products we sold.

I am not like the many successful businessmen who had paper rounds or countless get-rich-quick-schemes when they were young. I couldn't do that. I had no opportunities like that in Bangladesh. But I always had a plan and a firm idea of what my future held. I knew I would not work for anybody else; I always wanted to create something, some sort of business or new enterprise. I used to learn who does what, what is the best way to make money (the proper way of course).

When I saw the opportunity to make money, supplying foods instead of selling them in my father's shop, it was the moment I thought, 'At last I have my business.' I knew it was my chance. Sometimes you make so much money it encourages you to go for a bigger chunk and expand massively in all directions. I always preferred a niche market. I have always been creative; I always wanted to do something other people didn't do.

The shrimps most people were familiar with before the 1980s were just cocktail prawns. We introduced black tiger shrimps to Europe, which I branded Mr Prawn and Tiger Brand, because I was confident that my product was good and different. I always had Britain in particular, and Europe in general, in mind. They had never accepted cooked prawns from the Far East or from Asian countries before then. I took on the challenge to prove they could be popular, bringing prawns from Thailand, a country quite famous for its prawns in Asia. I have been involved with so many groups in Thailand and I love the skill they have in delivering them. I transferred that knowledge to the United Kingdom and then to Bangladesh.

I import shrimps and king prawns, and process them in the hi-tech machines here in Britain to British standards then export them back all over the world. It would not last if I had no factory in Bangladesh. Because for the last twenty years Bangladesh has become so developed, along with countries like India, Malaysia, Thailand, Indonesia and Vietnam, a lot of manufacturing business has gone abroad due to high manufacturing costs in the UK. So I thought if I don't go to India or Bangladesh or Thailand then I will lose this business, so I went to Bangladesh to set up a British investment with the help from the DTI and the British High Commission. They helped us a lot. I have huge processing and freezing facilities, particularly in Chittagong in Bangladesh. Many of the companies who have not done this have lost out. Basically, now we can sell from Bangladesh and Britain and our customers are happy. Otherwise I could have lost business. People would think, 'Why should I buy from you if the shrimps are coming from Bangladesh?' Now I can say, 'Well I can serve you from Bangladesh' or, 'I can serve you from England, wherever is convenient.' They run in tandem,that is one of the great advantages of being a citizen of two countries. Prawns and tiger prawns are a big thing but it is a very niche market.

When I opened my second factory in Droylsden, I knew a big supplier who was a member of a Thai group who had four or five factories in Thailand producing for one market and fulfilling huge demands in the USA. I asked him to take me to their consortium. He put me in touch with their group and the Walmart representative buyers visited my factories in Bangladesh and Manchester. When they came to Manchester they approved my factory and wanted to see the largest Tesco and the largest Sainsbury's in the country. So early in 2001, I took them to London to the giant Tesco in Cromwell Road and the next visit we made was to Oxford Street to Sainsbury's. They went there, saw the product and I asked, 'What do you think?' I was talking about the seafood in particular as well as other frozen goods. They looked at the frozen food and asked me about the products. I said, 'No, we are much better than this.'

A few months later, I was lucky enough to meet Lord Sainsbury at a function I was invited to at the House of Lords.

I said: 'Lord Sainsbury, I need to talk to you. . . ' I told him that I had had my factory inspected by Walmart buyers and they had wanted to see one of his largest stores: 'I took them, they saw your product and they said it was not up to their standards. They said your packaging is not good enough!' I was quite worried about what his reaction would be.

He gave me a pained smile and I said, 'Have I said something wrong?' He said, 'No, no, no, you are absolutely right.' It is the one thing I have said that I was proud of. In those days I was a member of the British Food Export Council.

I have always been very interested in the quality of everything. Quality control and all the issues are very important and so is talking to people about what they want. It was a gradual process, getting our prawns accepted by bigger and bigger outlets. We took it one step at a time and quality is always the most important factor. It still is today. We listen to our customers, we do exactly what the customer wants and we make sure all our staff are trained to take care of the product in the best way possible. The factories we've built are all 100 per cent approved to British standards and BRC accredited, and they all process in the British way. Another thing I have always done is to look after our own staff well. Their welfare is very important to me. I have always been fond of my staff. Some have left from time to time but most of them come back, because we treat them like members of our family.

I always feel proud to be the head of our 'family' of more than 4,000 people who work for me. If I can create one job I feel great. I make sure I choose the right candidate in the first place and I take my time about it. I don't say, 'Oh yes, you have got the job,' to any handsome man or pretty woman that comes along. We want talented, hard-working people. Those are the important qualities I am always looking for. We have a very clear system of assessing people. We want someone we can feel comfortable with and who can feel comfortable with us. But I do feel very upset if I lose one good worker.

We have about 350 employees in Manchester, a lot in Bangladesh and some in America and in other parts of the world. In Bangladesh we have more because they are processing and they are fishing in the Bay of Bengal. We have large fishing trawlers, they go out to sea for about one month catching fish and prawns and then freeze the fish at sea and come back; these stay frozen until they are eaten. Inside the factory in Bangladesh, we employ a lot of people, the majority of them females from the hill tracks who are educated and dedicated. But in England, we've got more machine processing so we don't need as many people. The product we import is semi-processed.

Let me explain what we do! We get the shrimps in Bangladesh, the heads are taken off, as are the shell skins; and only the meat part is frozen. They do a bulk pack, block frozen, so when it comes here it's already cleaned up and we can do the value addition. Value addition simply means adding ingredients. It could be a spice, it could be a sauce or just a salt. There are many other varieties.

Most of the shrimps no longer come from the Bay of Bengal. Most are cultivated now. But their mothers and fathers came from the Bay of Bengal! These days they are cultivated just offshore all over the world. All the big shrimps you get today are mostly cultivated. Now, I process more than a million prawns a minute as we expand. Communities are growing and we are also growing, more and more countries are importing from us. It's a huge market.

The seafood industry really started when Asian people came to the UK. It's not just the Bangladeshis, but people from China, the Philippines, Thailand, Japan, India and other countries. They love fish and rice. British people in the old days only used to like red meat. Then they started eating it in many different kinds of restaurants, which also sold shrimps and fish. And then the doctors came up with the theory that more seafood is good for you, and recommended cutting down on the red meat. The doctors were right of course, as well as extremely helpful! We were so fortunate! That helped us enormously and made it a beautiful start. Now if you go to the supermarket you see more shrimps, more seafood, more fish, value-added fish. It has been a constant expansion since we started and we're still expanding.

A business of our kind, especially as a service industry, can't stop. If you stop, you're dead. Somebody will overtake you. I'll give you an example: we introduced the Germans to shrimps. Before then, in that part of the world, and in France and Italy, they used to eat cold-water shrimps. We introduced the warm-water variety. The market for warm-water shrimps started growing because they are much tastier and so the market in cold-water shrimps began to decrease. That helped us enormously and we expanded the European market.

We have been serving customers in Europe for the past twenty-five years. It's a massive market and some of the customers have become bigger than me now, selling more seafood than I do! Twenty-five years ago we taught people how to sell. They did not know what tiger shrimps were.

Now they buy shrimps from us and from other parts of the world, from our competitors. So as you can imagine, the market has become huge. It is growing every day and we created that!

CHAPTER SEVENTEEN

USA SETBACK

We have a considerable business in the United States, but there is a reason we are not more successful there. For many years I was a regular visitor to one of the largest seafood shows in the USA, the Boston Seafood Show, which is held in March every year. I became interested in setting up a business in the USA. During this time, an organisation called Food From Britain (FFB), under the wing of the British Food Export Council, helped me to set up Seamark USA in Newark, New Jersey. The business was good and we were thinking of expanding on a larger scale.

But then 9/11 happened and everything went wrong for the business because most of the people working in the company were Asian. Morale was down. The events of that day in 2001 made it very difficult for Asian people to visit the United States. I used to get stopped in immigration all the time. I was always asked if I was from Pakistan because my name was blacklisted. At one point, I had to appoint an attorney to clear my name; I was even told by the FBI that I should change it! I refused to do that.

I remember I was travelling with the famous Bollywood actor Amitabh Bachchan and his wife Jaya Bhaduri one time. His wife passed through immigration but Amitabh and myself were stopped and were delayed for some time. The same thing happened to my son, Manzur. I am still running the business under the name Seamark USA Inc. We have a distribution centre and a cold storage facility there. Unfortunately, I could not fulfill my desire to expand as much as I wished.

CHAPTER EIGHTEEN

BANK STORY

Every business needs money to make it run. I was very fortunate when I started that so many of my father's friends generously invested in me. I paid them all back of course, but as I was building the business there were several times when I needed to borrow larger amounts of money to grow to the next level. I remember after we had built the cold store in the shop next door in Oldham (By then I was living some way away from the shop in a nice big house), I found I was short of money to expand the business.

I always kept on top of my own accounts, maintaining my ledger, which I had been taught years earlier by my mother. She was a great business lady, very meticulous, and she taught me at a very early age the importance of recording all my accounts. I always tell everybody that you should be your own bookkeeper. It keeps you on top of exactly where you are, it makes it all transparent. You can't tell a story to somebody unless you write it down, especially the figures. The story you can remember, but figures you can't. If you write everything down and every day or every week you make a balance and you can see what you have done. It was a simple system but it served me very well. One of my father's friends used to do the tax returns.

The business was full of potential but I needed a large investment to develop that potential. I had so much money coming in and the turnover and profit was growing slowly, but I didn't have capital. My father's friends could only give me a few thousand pounds, not the amount I really needed at this stage in the early 80s. So, I thought, 'I will have to go to the bank.'

My father's best friend was an accountant, a Bangladeshi guy, who used to do the accounts for lots of the restaurants. He firmly advised me more than once, 'You don't want to borrow money from banks. They will rip you off.' He always discouraged me. And my father said the same thing. He was very much against borrowing from banks or building societies. 'Your mortgage will never finish in this country,' he stated. In fact, everybody I spoke to was totally discouraging. And it was a very difficult time as the interest rate was 15 or 16 per cent back then in the late 80s. This was quite an unfamiliar problem for Bangladeshi people like my family. Back home we didn't pay mortgages or rent, because we already owned the houses! Unfortunately that was anything but the case in England, so I decided to ignore all the well-meaning advice and go ahead with trying to negotiate a loan from a bank.

I first went to the Yorkshire Bank by myself. I had heard they were the most conservative bank. They kicked me out very swiftly. Then I went to Lloyds Bank, which was also thought to be safe and conservative, and I was greeted with a firm 'No' to my request. My friend Khurshed Alam suggested I open an account with Barclays. 'First let me find out whether I know a manager,' Khurshed said. 'You need to know the manager to get anywhere with a bank!'

Time was passing now, and I was grimly counting, every day thinking, 'What is going to happen if I don't get the money I need? How am I going to establish my business without money?' Eventually Khurshed found someone called, amazingly to me, Mr Oldham. His office was in Ardwick Green, Manchester. Khurshed and I went round and he introduced me to Mr Oldham, a very tall older gentleman. We talked for a while about how much we needed to borrow and in the end he said, 'OK I'll come back to you.' We waited for three months but he never came back to me. Then one day I went past the bank and suddenly noticed a load of building work. It looked as if the bank was being demolished! There was a lot of scaffolding and stuff at the front and there was a temporary entrance.

By then we had made quite a lot of transactions. There was a good deal of cash coming in and going out and I thought we had a very good statement. I went in and I looked for Mr Oldham. There was no sign of him and the staff said he had been transferred and there was a new manager, called Stuart Pennell. 'OK,' I said to myself, 'this time I am calling to open a new account to borrow some money.' But I didn't get anywhere and had to make another appointment. The next time I tried my luck, the building work was still going on and there was a temporary bank in place, like a cabin. At the front was a girl cashier taking money in. This time I went with my brother Kamal. I let him out of the car as I went to find a parking space and he went in to deposit some money.

As I was going into the bank I couldn't believe what I saw. A black guy grabbed a bag of money from the girl and ran. I ran after him and chased him into a derelict area. Soon the police arrived. I was searching for the thief, but the policeman told me I shouldn't be taking the law into my own hands and that I could have been hurt. I was a bit upset. 'Bloody hell I'm trying to do a good deed,' I thought. When I came back everybody was complaining, but the girl was very sympathetic. The staff said, 'You don't have to do that. Often thieves are dangerous people.' I certainly learned a lesson that day. It was a bit embarrassing, I just ran after him without thinking. Later the story got out about a Pakistani guy (that was how they described me) running after the black guy who had snatched the girl's bag!

After all this excitement I finally went in to see the manager. I received another shock when I saw him: he was identical to the Russian leader, Mikhail Gorbachev, with a blotchy birthmark on his head. Before I could stop myself, I said. 'You look like Gorbachev!' He winced, saying, 'Everybody says that.' This was Stuart Pennell, who I had wanted to see for so long. I started to try to compose myself and to explain why I needed to borrow some money. I got my red Collins bookkeeping ledger out, to show him my figures. I don't think that was how ordinary businessmen behaved, and he was laughing gently at me. I didn't mind as he did it in a kind way.

He was impressed. My brother Kamal was sitting next to me and Stuart Pennell asked questions for fifteen or twenty minutes. Then he said, 'Do you have a balance sheet?' I was honest and said, 'I haven't done it for this year yet as the year is still in progress. You can see from my book how we are doing.' I added, 'Look, I can double or even triple the amount of sales and I can make real money.' After a while he talked to me then said, 'It's OK. How much you need?' I said, 'I need £50,000.' He said, 'Let's talk about £100,000!'

I was so happy, Stuart Pennell was like a second angel to me – the first were my father's friends who helped me to get really going in business. I still think it was probably because I ran after that bugger!

CHAPTER NINETEEN

BUYING A
WAREHOUSE

In 1984 I had ambitions to buy a warehouse. I wanted to buy one in Manchester right next to the wholesale market. I was keen to establish a base on the same road so that I could attract customers from the perishable market. It sounds simple enough but in fact it was very difficult. Why? Number one: I was young. Number two: I think people looked at me and wondered: 'Has he got the money?' We saw a signboard for a 5,500-square-foot warehouse for sale. I struggled to find out how much it was selling for. I was ringing the agent and bargaining and getting nowhere. I had the feeling that if I had been a white, older English man then I would have fared much better.

Somehow I found out the gentleman who owned the warehouse was called Anthony Preston and I decided to go and see him. At the time I had a 190E Mercedes that I had just bought brand new. It was a great-looking car, black with a low suspension. I thought it would create a good impression.

I intentionally drove right into the loading bay, which I knew perfectly well I was not supposed to do. I wanted him to see the car, I wanted people to see my car. I asked to see Mr Preston. He soon appeared and he was a smart gentleman. 'Can we sit down? I need to talk to you,' I said. We sat together in a small canteen and he asked me very politely what he could do for me.

I explained I was keen to buy his warehouse and I was not getting anywhere with the agent. I remembered something I learned from my grandmother: 'Tell people the important truth. Tell them everything.' I told Mr Preston the truth, which was that his warehouse was vital to me. I told him my business was going so well I really needed a warehouse. I didn't see any warehouse better than his. He was asking for £90,000. I said, 'I can make a deal. I have no problem with the cash. I am not going to waste time, but the important thing is I will be grateful to you forever, because this is the place I need.' He said, 'Have you got the money?'

I offered £80,000. He said: 'No, I'm asking £90,000.' He was looking at me. I could see he was a nice man, and in fact I still know him. He led me outside as we talked. I knew his intention was to see my car. The black Mercedes looked impressive. Lovely car,' he said, then added, 'How about meeting in between.' In that time I think he made a judgment about me. I think he liked my approach and believed in me. We agreed on £85,000, and shook hands on the deal. He said, 'How soon can you come in? I want to move out as soon as possible?'

I was very heartened by the deal and it was very important to me. I believe it was racist attitudes that prevented me getting through to Mr Preston. Whether it was or not, when you approach a decent person directly and properly then racism disappears and you become two honest men doing a fair deal.

CHAPTER TWENTY

SUCCESS

The money I received from Stuart Pennell, and the warehouse from Anthony Preston, were two huge leaps forward for me. This was the middle of the 1980s and I truly believe my success story started then. A sum of £100,000 was like a £1,000,000 nowadays. From then onwards I started making real money, from the warehouse. It really moved me up a gear, but there were still problems ahead, sadly some of them to do with the colour of my skin!

I wanted to build a larger cold-storage warehouse and this when I came across discrimination. I couldn't buy land. I couldn't convert an old building. I needed a new purpose-built structure because I needed a certain height and insulation panels. So it made sense to design it myself; new build seemed a much better route forward than trying to adapt some old building. Then it was like hitting a brick wall: I couldn't get land. I tried everything, but whatever I tried I was faced with a lot of problems, particularly with planning permission. I had to spend a lot of money searching for the right piece of land and then I realised that Manchester City Council thought I could not build an attractive building so they were not confident in giving me planning permission or selling me land.

I couldn't understand why my attempts to build a new cold-storage warehouse, which would create business and jobs for the area, were constantly thwarted. I consulted with an architect and designer called Jonathan Bolchover, a close and trusted friend of my family. He was frank with me and told me bluntly, 'You won't get planning permission.'

Jonathan and his wife Joyce are both architects. They are Jewish and are familiar with all the subtleties of racism. I was angry about the decisions of the council and others. Jonathan recommended a solicitor who suggested the only way to progress my idea was to ask a builder to design and build, and as soon as the project was finished, to have it in a contract that it was handed over to me. I talked to the architect/designer who gave the builder the specification. My name was kept completely out of the arrangement.

So I had to hire somebody else and I knew I needed somebody who was white-skinned and British, rather than Asian and brown-skinned like myself. I hired a builder called Mr Knight, of Knight Holdings Ltd, from Nottingham, who fitted the bill, to proceed as if it was his own project. I saw a corner plot of empty land for sale, a unit. In 1989 I went to meet Mr Knight and told him exactly what my problem was. I asked him to buy the land and to build for me.

We paid Knight Holdings through our solicitors. That's the way I built the building. We paid everything. That is how we were able to build our warehouse.

Racism exists not only in London or Manchester or anywhere in Great Britain: it is all over the world. As soon as you say I'm from England, they look at you and say, 'You don't look like you are from England.' I am from England. I live there and I've got a British passport. My business is based there. My children are all British and born in England. That is the initial task you have to go through. People used to laugh at me. Nowadays, the first question is: 'Where are you from?' 'England,' I answer. The second question: 'Where do you come from originally?' I say: 'My family comes from Bangladesh.' If you ask my son he will not answer you. He will say: 'I am from England, I was born here.'

My brother went to Milan in the late 1990s and he was entertaining one of our customers. After a few drinks they were asking, 'Are you from Bangladesh? How come you live in England? Do you really have a factory in Manchester?' They couldn't believe it. They could not believe he was British. 'Yes we have a factory in England,' he said. 'We don't believe you,' they said. 'You must be importing and storing the product in England and supplying from there.' My brother said, 'No, no we have our own factory.' But they would not believe him. He called me and told me this guy didn't believe we had a factory. I said, 'Why don't you offer them a business-class return ticket. I'll pay for it. Tell them to come and see me and I'll show them round our factory.' Although at first it can be quite difficult to convince people we really are British, which can be irritating and frustrating, we never give up.

An Asian lord, who is a professor, was speaking and I went to listen. I raised my hand to ask a question: 'I'm a businessman and I sometimes find it difficult to promote my business in

England because people don't trust me. I am British and I can maintain British standards of honesty, so what do I do?'

He said: 'The simple way is you put English people in front of you and stay behind.' So the easy answer was to hire English people and let them do it for you, which I did. In the early days we hired them to be our sales executive and marketing PR officer. He told me, change your company name, don't mention Iqbal anywhere, because that is your first mistake, people think it is an Asian company. Thankfully, those days have gone, but we did create a new company: Seamark, short for Seafood Marketing International Ltd. It is not a Bangladeshi name but a British name.

To me it doesn't matter where you from. You have to be smart. You have to feel international. In the old days, if your approach wasn't right then acceptance wasn't there, but now if the approach is right you are accepted. Now I don't feel any difficulties anywhere in the world. Generally that's gone. Enoch Powell was forgotten a long time ago. Racism no longer exists at the same level it did in the past. There are people who still have fear, when they don't need to. They should be confident about doing business anywhere in the world.

CHAPTER TWENTY-ONE

ALEC DODGEON

B usiness is all about people and you can meet great people who can become employees in the strangest places. In the old days the bank manager used to be very powerful. I was with Barclays Bank in Ardwick for several years. I stayed for five years and then another manager came along and I didn't get on with him. That branch closed down and was moved to Levenshulme – imagine having to move banks! I was not pleased, but it turned out very well for this is when I met Alec Dodgeon. He was the manager at Levenshulme. In those days he was a great manager. That was in the mid-1980s.

In 1991 he gave me £600,000 to further expand as the demand for tiger prawns grew and grew. Alec was very wise and understanding because that was during the recession.

The £600,000 formed part of the capital needed to build our first factory in Whitworth Street in Manchester. I was ambitious, I wanted to build my own factory. He sanctioned the money, I built the factory and after two years we opened and Alec was one of my guests at the opening ceremony. He had retired from the bank by then, because Barclays had centralised everything. Alec was only fifty-four.

So after two years I called him and I offered him a job and he was so delighted. He started part-time, a few days only, and then he gradually became full-time. Without him having qualifications in accountancy, I made him my financial controller. He was good at arithmetic. He was good at drafting letters. I learned a great deal from him and he was with me for several years and became my best friend. He travelled with me all over the world. I gave him another career and he became a very valued colleague. I think it changed his life, and I would like here to give Alec the chance to recall our association:

"I retired for the second and final time at the end of January 2008. I had first retired much earlier, but Iqbal provided an exhilarating finale to my career. I was there as his amazing business really flourished and I wouldn't have missed it for the world. Nowadays I live quietly in the countryside in the north of England and fondly remember my hectic final years of work. My wife comes from Carlisle and she always said she wanted to come back when the children had grown up and gone their separate ways. It is very peaceful up here, not at all like life with Iqbal Ahmed!

I enjoyed my time with Iqbal very much. I first met him in October 1985 when I became manager of Barclays Bank in Levenshulme, Manchester. He was then one of our bigger wholesale customers. I was very impressed by him the first time we met. It was clear from the start that he was meticulous.

He was not the easiest customer to get along with because I think he felt he had a lot of responsibility on his shoulders. He always wanted to control every detail of the expanding business himself and unless he was away he wouldn't let his brother Kamal take over control of anything. He always wanted everything just so, just right.

He was quite a young man when I met him. Kamal was a bit younger and their youngest brother Bilal was a wee lad! I got on very well with Kamal and Bilal, particularly Kamal. He doesn't talk a lot. But he thinks quite deeply about things. When Iqbal goes away he is not quite happy to leave day-to-day affairs in his brother's control, yet Kamal always does a good job. He is very able in his own right.

The younger brothers always seemed extremely happy to have Iqbal as their leader. I think it's partly their culture, where the oldest brother is in charge. Their loyalty and devotion to Iqbal is quite remarkable. They are a very warm and close family and they were always extremely good to work with. After their father died quite a few years ago, Iqbal assumed total responsibility for the family, looking after his mother and to a certain extent his sisters.

By the time we met in 1985 he had built up quite a business. He had started off in Oldham in Sickle Street where his father had a corner shop. And they had the house next door. When his father retired, Iqbal decided he didn't want to be serving behind a counter for the rest of his life. He would do something else. He realised that the growing number of Asian restaurants and shops in the area needed supplies and he asked himself, 'What do they need?' The main thing they needed was fish. There was a scarcity of prawns and shrimps and because of his contacts in Bangladesh he knew where he could get them. So he filled the shop and the house next door.

He filled it with the biggest freezers he could buy. They were enormous great things. That's how they started. I think they then moved out to the premises in Openshaw up the main road into Manchester. Anyway, they still got the shop in Sickle Street. They turned it into a shop and his sister runs it up to this day.

I came on the scene during the time when he wanted to develop a plot of land on Ashton Old Road in Manchester. The developer had planning permission for three units and Iqbal said, 'I don't want three units. I want one big one,' and he managed to get the permission changed. We helped to finance it and this was the first big cold store he had.

My initial impression of Iqbal when he first walked in was very favourable. He was introduced to me by Stuart Pennell, the previous manager of the bank, who spoke very highly of him. My impression was good too. He seemed to have a very clear idea of what he was doing. He was ambitious and he knew exactly where he was going, but he was not reckless. Iqbal didn't do anything without thinking about it quite deeply and going into the ramifications and the effects and the consequences. So I was confident he would be successful. I remember he did have an accountant who was a Bangladeshi like himself. And he was like a father figure to him because Iqbal's father had gone back to Bangladesh by then I had to persuade him in due course to move to the traditional firm of Royce Peeling Green. They are good people and they're still there.

Seamark was Seafood Marketing International Ltd originally. He liked to impress people with the international side of it. As a marketing name, Iqbal Brothers didn't sound too impressive. He is very conscious of image and impression, very much so. So I was helpful to him initially in two ways: for the loan for the new premises and in recommending a new accountant. I got the accounts in order, got the cash flow sorted out and the projections and so on, and without much difficulty we got the loan through and that was that – he marched on from there.

I left my job on 1 October 1991. The bank was going through a big change. It was getting rid of virtually every middle and senior management person who was aged over fifty and I was one of them. Under the radical reorganisation my branch was clustered into a group of about four I think, under the control of somebody else. I think Iqbal at that stage had forged a relationship with a new executive at the bank and in due course he had access to senior management in Manchester. The local director in charge of business, John Allen, had a good relationship with Iqbal, but in the end the business went elsewhere. These things happen. There was no rancour or ill will; it was just that Iqbal and I got the deal we wanted from somebody else. All things being equal that's the way you go. Even I, as an ex-Barclays man, had no qualms about it whatsoever.

So having been Iqbal's bank manager for about six years, I had a break of about four. I was fifty-four when I retired and I stayed retired until Iqbal asked me to work for him. I was enjoying my retirement. I still had children at home but hadn't any grandchildren, and I was very much involved with family. I thought I had finished with work.

He invited me to the opening of the new premises on Ashton Old Road, in 1993, which I had helped to finance.

It was opened by the High Commissioner for Bangladesh, who came up from London, and John Gummer, then the Minister for Agriculture, Fisheries and Food. There were two premises. The original Iqbal Brothers was on the corner, just a cold store, and at the end of the same block, about 200 yards away, was the new much larger grander and more effective premises. In this bigger unit was not only a big cold store but also a very intricately designed freezing unit. Because the premises was not really as big as Iqbal would have liked, he formed a relationship with a Danish food-machinery manufacturer called Carnitech a relationship that exists to this day. He's done a lot with Carnitech and they've done a lot with him. And that really got him going on the production side because otherwise they would have had to just buy in and wouldn't have been able to process their own products. That gave him the opportunity for vertical integration, a further step forward.

At the opening Iqbal said, 'I've got a part-time job going as financial controller two or three days a week. Do you fancy it?' I thought, 'That sounds good.' I must have been on his mind; he doesn't forget his friends. I said the job sounded interesting and asked him, 'What do you want me to do?' He said, 'Well I've got an office here. I've got a room, and all the rest of the staff work in a room. I haven't got any room for you really. When somebody gets up and goes you can use their desk!' I joined him in February 1996, as the Financial Controller. We survived, though sometimes it was a squeeze.

It was a good team. Executive assistant, Nita Shah, one of Iqbal's longest serving people, was there, of course. I always got on well with her. She is a very smart young lady.

2015 – with the Business Person of the Year Award at the Asian Achievers Awards, held at Grosvenor House, Park Lane, London.

Above: 2001 – handing out gifts to factory workers in Bangladesh.

Below: Receiving the National Export Trophy 2006–7 from the Prime Minister of Bangladesh, Sheikh Hasina, at a ceremony in Dhaka, 11 March 2010.

Above: 2011 – with Baroness (Sayeeda) Warsi and other members of the Conservative Party during a visit to the Burunga Iqbal Ahmed High School and College in Sylhet, Bangladesh.

Below: 2014 – speaking as a member of the panel of the 10th WIEF (World Islamic Economic Forum), Dubai.

Above: In 1999 Seamark won the inaugural Business in Europe Award.

Below: 2013 – at the Burunga Iqbal Ahmed High School and College with (from left to right) Rushanara Ali MP, Shabana Mahmood MP and Shofiqul Islam, school principal.

Above: With David Cameron, the then Prime Minister, at my Vermilion Restaurant in Manchester, 5 January 2012.

Below: 2010 – attending a formal dinner at the Lancaster Hotel, London.

Above left: At Liverpool University in 2012 for my only son Manzur's graduation ceremony for his MBA.

Above right: 2009 – at Manchester University with my son, wife and mother for the graduation of my youngest daughter, Hamida.

Below: With my wife and daughters at Manchester Town Hall for the wedding of my son, Manzur, to Sarah, September 2015.

Above left: 2015 – with my granddaughters, Parisa and Amira.

Above right: With Amma, my mother, on a summer's day at home in Cheshire.

Below: Family holiday in Monaco in August 2016, with my wife, daughter Shahida, son-in-law Mahi, and grandchildren Parisa and Amira.

2005 – with my son, Manzur, in the garden at home.

I discovered that the business had not grown vastly. But it was about to. This was the take-off point and I think Iqbal felt, in fairness to me, that he needed someone with a bit of professional expertise. He also knew it would be good to have a European among his senior team! He was keen on Europe. He had toeholds in Italy and France, Germany and Belgium. He wanted to expand those and I think he felt that having me with him from time to time when meeting customers would perhaps give them a bit of assurance that he was solid and reliable, which, of course, he was. I had no qualms about helping him.

Of course when I started there was no question of the job just being two or three days a week. It was immediately full-time. I was financial controller. I don't think racial discrimination was a factor at that point, though I think it did help to have a solid English bank manager on his team. I never experienced any racial problems myself. To me a chap is as good as his word. Iqbal always, to my mind, did what he said he would. He is very conscious of wanting to show his own family and his own people in the UK and in Bangladesh how well he has done. He wanted to make sure they knew that he had climbed a long way up the tree.

Iqbal was anxious at that time to expand the business because he had an appetite for production. He was very proud of that small unit because it initially posed a few problems – it needed a production line that could go round corners – and Carnitech had it said it could not be done. Iqbal said, 'Yes you've got to do it.' So they said, 'OK, we'll think about it.' Then they came back and said, 'Yeah, we've worked something out. We think we can get it round here and round here. . . ' It was for prawns, which he had not processed before. Although he had a cold store, other people had to process them in Bangladesh or in India or wherever he could buy them. He wanted to do the processing. He wanted to buy the raw product because there was a big demand for it.

Iqbal was the guy who introduced the king prawn to Europe. It is now big business. One part of my job was to go to the bankers and another was to look for possible sites. I was trawling the net just like some of the fishermen he employs. We were looking at another site quite near to where this building was on Ashton New Road and then the Johnstone's pain factory site came up. Johnstone's were taken over by somebody or other and they decided to move the entire business to their HQ in Wakefield. They had asked for planning permission to put a bridge over the canal to connect to a piece of land they wanted to develop and Manchester City Council, in their wisdom, decided not to allow it. So Johnstone's said, 'Right, blow you! We'll close the place down.' So it came up for sale. We looked at the place and thought, 'Yes, it's a good size. It's a cracking size. It just needs converting. Can it be done?'

All the floors were OK and the height and the doors. The access was fine. The place needed a thorough renovation, of course. In effect, we had to build a new factory inside the old one. That was what happened. We had new walls and a new roof. We had to put in an entirely new substation. Whilst the site was ideal in many ways and the buildings were good, they needed a 100 per cent conversion effort because they had been used for producing paint; some of it was toxic and we had to turn it into a proper food-production unit. Financially, this was a big leap forward. This is where Barclays helped (this was still in the Barclays era). I haven't a clue the overall figure of the cost. The potential was to more than double – more like multiply by five times – the size of the business. The production line was big; it was a big unit.

If it wasn't prosperous with money being retained the bank wouldn't have been interested. You had to show your cash flows and your budget projections had to be vetted very carefully. We gave our accountants the basics and I went through it with them and made sure it all made sense. Of course a lot of that sense was really Iqbal's amazing ability to generate the high level of business he said he could. And which, of course, he did.

Iqbal was still banking with Barclays when I joined him. At some stage, when we bought out Johnstone's on Edge Lane, which took some doing and cost a lot of money, we needed more money. Barclays began began raising questions and whatnot, so we then thought of possible alternatives. We had friends in HSBC – I'm sure Iqbal will remember the phrase, 'friends across the road'– whom I called. We went to HSBC and they said, 'No problem'. So we decided to go with them. I presume he still is. It's good to have a banking friend in reserve when you're in business. You never know when they might be needed, as indeed they were.

If I had to assess Iqbal as a businessman I would rate him very, very highly. He is extremely decisive and clear-thinking. He is a natural born leader, in my view. The whole astonishing enterprise was his vision from the start. I suspect that if Kamal had been the older one it might have been a different story. Iqbal is one of the best organisers that you will ever meet. He'll organise anything. In fact, given half a chance, before you know it he will take over the organising for you, even though he may have no particular need to. He just has that sort of mind. If we had a dinner party or a social event, he would organise all the placings and tiny details, things like that on whatever he thought would work. He is a perfectionist. He likes everything to be just right and plans and prepares everything down to the last detail. You could say he was quite controlling, and to a degree that is absolutely true. I don't think he would have got where he was had he not been. He wants to know everything and doesn't delegate easily. When at times he was quite happy to delegate, I always had to report back on every detail.

The Johnstone's paint plant deal was the first big thing I undertook as financial controller. That was when I got my own office. We employed a full-time qualified accountant in the office and the sales staff were all based there. Kamal had an office near mine. The deal transformed the business. It meant we could import a great deal more shrimps and prawns and process them ourselves and sell a great deal more. It made a heck of a difference. It meant that our annual turnover went from about a few millions to tens of millions a year. It didn't happen overnight. It was quite visionary for Iqbal to see the potential in turning a paint factory into a food-processing unit.

It was a good unit and it served us well. The scope of the original processing unit was limited. It could only do so many tons a week whereas this new unit could do ten times more. And the cold store was vast, a huge thing, not as big as the one we were to build at Miles Platting, mind you, but it was big.

I think the planning rows were largely over by the time I arrived. I thought he got on well with the local authority. He knew Howard Bernstein, now chief executive on Manchester City Council. He likes to know people who it is important to know. His local MP at the time was our now chancellor, George Osborne, and Iqbal had the foresight to invite him to the opening of the first phase of the new plant in Miles Platting.

Iqbal was particularly keen to include a restaurant cum nightspot, which became Vermilion, and Miguel Cancio Martins came along. He was Portuguese, an interior designer of international renown. He was based in Paris and highly recommended. If you want to do a restaurant he is the man, having created all sorts of restaurants in capital cities. He was very interesting, about 6ft 2in, with curly brown hair and piercing blue eyes. I think there was a strong Irish ancestry. He was good. Iqbal and I had our budget. We had difficulty in controlling Miguel who wanted it done his way all the time, he had to have the best. Iqbal and I wanted to keep costs under control but he insisted on manmade polished granite in the bathrooms that was very expensive. A similar product was half the price. 'Oh we can use this,' we said. 'You can't,' he insisted.

Iqbal is very warm and hospitable. He is always very conscious of taking care of guests who should be looked after properly. He likes good food. I went to a party at his house once and I remember and he said, 'Those of you who want a drink, you're over in the pavilion in the garden.' Iqbal's son Manzur has been groomed to take over one day. Iqbal keeps an eye on him but Manzur is very able and a real chip off the old block."

Thank you Alec. What happy memories you bring back to me! You are one of the people who have been important to me. And, given that Alec was involved at the start, it may be useful to mention here how the company's premises have expanded over the years.

We had a very successful period in our first factory in Whitworth Street, which we also referred to as 'Seamark 1'. But we were, as we call it, under production. There was a huge demand for our product from Europe; our exports were almost 85–90 per cent. We needed another factory, a bigger one. We were offered a brown-field site in Park House Street, Openshaw, by the council, so I created a scheme with the help of my architect, Jonathan Bolchover and his associates and a group of engineers.

I spent a lot of money putting the plans together but when we submitted the proposal for my project to the city council, it was rejected for various reasons. I was very disappointed and felt discriminated against. Even though I had made a success of Seamark 1, I could not convince the council that I could build a better factory and create more jobs. After a couple of days I told Alec that I did not think I could construct a brand-new building in Manchester so I would have to buy an old building to adapt for my new factory.

I did not want to waste more time. We started looking and put Alec on the case. He called some estate agents around Manchester and found one in Tameside who was marketing the Johnstone's Paints site in Droylsden, Manchester. It was perfect. It had storage and production facilities and a huge office building. As the seller was already in discussion with a French company, we got in touch with the top management, and I even talked to the Chairman. I negotiated and bought the place in 1997.

The site was huge. Both Alec and Kamal were worried about how on earth we were going to fill this place up, for it had over 150,000 square feet, four times more than our requirement. We converted the place and within three years the entire area was full. It had two to three shrimp-processing lines, value-added breaded line, value-added poultry line, three large cold-storage units, other storage areas, and the offices were all occupied.

The converted site in Droylsden, referred to as 'Seamark 2', was running at full capacity. Export was booming, but again we were running out of space. The three already large cold storages were at their full capacity. I remained hungry, more ambitious. I wanted a much bigger place. Luckily, I had a visitor from Midas one day, a friend called Neil Fountain. Midas is one of the agencies that promote inward investment in the city.

Neil was aware how disappointed I had been when my proposal for Park House Street was declined. The purpose of his visit was to find out whether I would be interested in investing in industrial sites that had become vacant after demolition of existing buildings. At the time the Manchester Authority was regenerating East Manchester and looking for investors, and I realised that this could not have come at a better time. To Neil I said, I am interested, but the choice has to be mine, to which he agreed.

So I drove around and saw a site between Lord North Street and Alan Turing Way, which was to become our corporate head office. It is a few hundred metres away from the Manchester City Football ground. Neil convinced me to go for it and said that he would negotiate with the council for me. I agreed to invest, but on the condition that I would not pay any money and instead spend it on my proposal subject to approval of the project. Then I would buy, which is what happened.

I must express my appreciation to Neil Fountain and his team at Midas for their help and assistance. This time the city council recognised my contribution and my capability to build and construct a factory in Manchester. With the project approved, I went for finance and construction began. In two and a half years' time the building was finished. It was built by one of the best builders in the country, Allenbuild, and by the end of 2005 IBCO Ltd moved, in followed by Seamark in summer 2008.

It is now the Seamark Group corporate head office. Within the site is a huge cold storage unit, one of the largest in the North-West of England, a cash-and-carry called Restaurant Wholesale, and the famous Vermilion restaurant. We are also currently constructing one of the best and largest wedding/function halls in the UK in the building that houses Vermilion. Named The Vermilion Hall, it can cater for anything from 250 up to 1,000 people. I still have an option to build a four star hotel within the site. Perhaps, in the near future, it is something that I will definitely consider.

Another man who was immensely valuable was called Graham Thorpe. He was a speaker at a seminar I attended. I have always been thirsty for knowledge. No one is born knowing everything he needs to know. I believe you have to keep learning all your life. When you think you know everything it's probably time to call it a day!

I used to attend quite a few seminars. They became a very important thing in my life because I do like to learn and to get involved with people. I met Mr Thorpe when I attended a seminar at the Salford regional head office of Barclays Bank. The bank sent me an invitation to listen to an information session called 'How to create funding for your organisation.' This was shortly after I had been given the vital overdraft by Stuart Pennell. That was the fund I needed to import the goods, but now that I was trying to export the goods I found I needed more funds. Where was I going to get the funds because I needed £1 million? I didn't have that kind of money, and I knew I couldn't make such a large amount of money that quickly.

So I went to the seminar and there was this very articulate and obviously intelligent Scottish guy with a little beard talking and about twenty of us listening. He was delivering a dissertation on how to raise funds for export and it was all very cosy. I kept finding I needed more explanation because I didn't understand the details of what he was saying. Every time he paused to go to a new item I raised my hand and asked a question. I raised my hand a lot. Eventually he said, 'Mr Ahmed can you please make note of all your questions and see me later on. I can explain everything.' I think he was getting fed up. But I was excited. I knew he was telling me some easy ways to make money for exports, but I didn't understand the details.

After the seminar he said, 'Right, let's go and have a coffee and I'll try to explain.' We went out of the area as he suggested and he asked me about my business. He wanted to know everything. He was a consultant to Barclays. We talked for a while and then he said, 'Come and see me tomorrow at ten o'clock, I'll help you.'

When I arrived, he was waiting for me, with four people, to help explain the details of the government's export credits guarantee department (ECGD). I still didn't find the details that easy to absorb but basically this government agency charged you one and a half per cent of your invoice value and then guaranteed to pay you 90 per cent of your invoice value.

It was also called credit insurance and it worked wonderfully for me. ECGD was created by the government at just around that time and I was probably its first customer. It was quite complicated but it helped me enormously and the business really started to grow.

I must also mention Dr David Carter, also a very influential man in my life. I got into a lot of trouble when I went to set up my factory in Bangladesh. However, as it was a British investment, I had support from the British government. David Carter was one of the most successful High Commissioners in Bangladesh, and he and his team at the British High Commission helped me enormously. With their advice and assistance I was able to obtain major trade licences, as well as securing EU approval, because I wanted to export to the EU. When I was ready to open the factory in 2000, I said to him: 'Look, David, as a British investor I want a British dignitary to open my factory.'

After a while David called me up and I went to see him. 'I've got good news,' he said. 'Somebody very important is coming to Bangladesh.' It was HRH Princess Anne, the Princess Royal. She opened my factory in November 2000 and David Carter was the man who made it happen. It was such a wonderful stamp of approval and I was absolutely delighted. The publicity was huge. Alec Dodgeon and David Mason, my bank manager at the time, were there alongside me. My wife Salma, family members and many high-profile dignitaries were among the guests as well as visitors from Britain.

Princess Anne was enchanting, a very nice person. She took the job seriously and showed great interest in the factory. I could not have asked for a better person to open it. We were told in advance, 'Oh, she is not going to do this. She is not going to do that. She is not going to give a speech or anything.' In fact when it came to it, she did everything. She was on the factory floor and she was talking to people so naturally, it was marvellous. It was a great boost for my business and I will be forever grateful to her and to David for helping to arrange it.

The royal opening gave my new factory great credibility and really made everyone sit up and take notice. It was a great part of my history.

CHAPTER TWENTY-TWO

CHARITY

There is a wonderful tradition in the country of my birth of helping others. The Bangladesh I was born into was not a country of great wealth. My family was comparatively well off as landowners with a large comfortable home, while most of our neighbours were not nearly so fortunate. But with that relative wealth came great unspoken responsibility. It was always clear to me growing up that as one of the most prominent families it was up to us to help others from time to time and that is what we did. My grandmother particularly was always vigilant in noticing any local hardship and always quick to offer a neighbourly hand of assistance when and where it would be most welcome.

From my childhood, charity was always on my mind. It was part of my life to do what English people call 'good turns' for others. It could have been anything from running a helpful errand to handing out a desperately needed loan that was never likely to be repaid. But it was a responsibility that has never gone away; over my years of doing business I have always helped people. I never run away from any problem that my friends or my neighbours might have. I don't have to think about what to do. Helping people has always been in my blood, and it is one of the biggest pleasures in my life.

When I was a little boy I remember how much we assisted people. We were often building things in the village. There was much cooperation involved and my father always made sure we went and volunteered. It was very much a family tradition. It was customary that out of three brothers only one brother had a job and the other two just made sure everybody got the work done and the kettles filled. It was not a hard life, and they always got invited to solve any problems in the union council, the local board. They were like social workers, so as I say, helping others has always been in our family blood.

My earliest recollections of charity work are of a great many small incidents. I used to do a lot of shopping for older people who found it difficult to get out. That was usually a weekly task. Also I recall accompanying many a lady who wanted to go to the hospital or to see a doctor. That was an everyday job. My mother also encouraged us to be very proactive in helping people. We were taught to keep an eye on our neighbours. If an older person was not seen out for a while we would go round and make sure they were OK.

Of course witnessing the massacre at Burunga High School changed everything in our lives. The peaceful village existence was smashed to smithereens. During the Liberation War and the terror and violence that entered our lives, I helped a lot of my school friends. When the soldiers started harassing and killing Hindus, almost at random, two or three of my friends from Hindu families took shelter in our house for a time. They were in fear of their lives and I helped them to cross the river and run away in case the army returned. I helped quite a few young Hindus by hiding them in the house. It was very dangerous. If the army had discovered them they could have taken action against me and my family. We would probably have been killed, but these were our friends. Our whole family felt that we had to help.

As I explained, this was a terrible time. Even before the massacre the soldiers used to take the young girls, and sometimes young boys, to their camp and they were never seen again.

When I came to England the war was still going on. It continued until the following year. Ordinary people joined the Liberation Army, called the Mukti Bahini, fighting for the freedom of Bangladesh. Young boys and men from all walks of life went out to fight the Pakistan army. During that time a huge financial contribution came from Bangladeshis Britain. People used to send their full salary to their friends and families in Bangladesh. In Greater Manchester there were a lot of Bangladeshi community leaders; indeed, my father was one of them. They led the way in organising the contributions as conditions worsened back home. I also helped my father to raise money in different ways. We had many charitable meetings and raised a considerable amount of cash. The money went from Britain to the border in India where the main Bangladeshi camp was located. The Liberation Army used to get it from there and buy clothes, food, arms and whatever they needed to fight, with the money. Later I was told many times that this money provided a vital lifeline.

Charity is a part of me, an important part. When I went to

London I used to help others even during my student time. Once I had learned to speak English properly, I would teach other students who were new to the country. I volunteered to help them learn the language, and guide them in where to live, how to behave and how to adopt the culture, to teach them about British society. That has always been a part of my life's routine work, and it continues.

One of the biggest fund-raising efforts I undertook was in 1991 when Bangladesh was hit by the deadliest cyclone on record. A huge flood left 138,000 people dead and another 10 million homeless. It was a natural catastrophe on the scale of the Japanese tsunami and other major disasters. There was international awareness of the disaster. I was well established in business by then and I decided I would raise funds.

Long-term employee Nita Shah was there and as usual she was brilliant. Yasmin, another long-term member of staff, was also a great help and Jim Carpenter of course. Those three were very important in my life over many years and particularly at this time. It is great to have that dedication from people you can turn to in a crisis and really trust. They helped me with the collection of all the donations and sending of funds to the cyclone-affected areas.

In such a situation raising money is only part of the solution. We also moved in a great deal of emergency supplies – food, tents, blankets and all sorts of equipment. It was very important that we maintained our support for the people, many of whom had lost everything in the disaster. There were many heart-rending personal stories of loss. It was a terrible time for so many of my people. And there was a cruel aftermath. When the flood had gone, we discovered there was, ironically, an alarming and very dangerous shortage of drinkable water. All the fresh water came from India, but for a time people could not consume that rainwater because so much of it was contaminated. There was very little mineral water available. Fresh clean water was very important. People were drinking all this dirty water and getting sick and dying. We decided to put in 500 fresh wells to access fresh water and improve the sanitisation. That provided swift and effective relief. My father was in Bangladesh at the time and he helped me a great deal.

In the UK I raised a lot of money and approached a lot of people to help set up a Business Link service with Bangladesh; I raised nearly £100,000. Then I went to Bangladesh and I met high commissioner at the time, Sir Colin Imray. 'I have raised £100,000,' I said. 'Have you got any ideas about how to distribute this money. Probably you can help me?' He was an Old Rotarian so he suggested the Rotary Club might be the best people to help as you can do a lot of charity work through them. Sylhet, my home district, was very much affected, and Sylhet Midtown Rotary Club and the club's president was one of my colleagues. So I went to meet him, a nice man, and organised a lot of much-needed acts of charity in-Medinapur, a village nearby.

I did a lot of different projects with the £100,000 but let me recall one of them. Together with a journalist, Mr Mahiuddin Shiru, who was a professor, and my father, we carried out some water rehabilitation and sanitation programmes, providing about 500 freshwater deep wells.

One of my good friends, Imran Ahmed MP also helped. This project was specially commended by Sir Colin Imray and was organised by a gentleman with a very similar name to my own, Iqbal U Ahmed. We've done a lot of projects together helping people. I remember him because he was a senior manager in AB Bank in those days, who then became a managing director of the Trust Bank. Iqbal U Ahmed became my best friend and he has helped me a great deal in setting up NRB Bank Limited. I am proud to include a few of his thoughts here.

CHAPTER TWENTY-THREE

IQBAL U AHMED SAYS

Iqbal Ahmed <u>OBE is</u> a generous person and a very good friend. I had an opportunity to get to know him through charity. He is <u>to me a so</u>cially responsible person with philanthropic orientation. As far as my memory goes, it was in the month of August 1992, when I was working as the area manager of AB Bank Ltd of Sylhet Division and the branches located across the Sylhet region were within my jurisdiction.

This posting had also given me the opportunity to come close to the inhabitants of Sylhet and to be acquainted with their cultural and social dynamics. In that year, Sylhet witnessed a devastating flood mainly a result of torrential rainfall and influx of water from the upstream Indian river in Meghalaya state. This devastating flood had rendered a large section of inhabitants of north-eastern region of Bangladesh and the *haor* (large water reservoir) area of greater Sylhet homeless and virtually marooned. In my personal capacity I was associated with some of the welfare-oriented organisations and at the same time I happened to be the president of Rotary Club of Sylhet Midtown. During this crisis period the club had taken initiatives to provide all required supports and assistance to the distressed people by way of distributing daily necessities and water-purifying tablets. A permanent solution for providing fresh drinking water through the building of tube wells was installed as the drinking-water crisis during the period had taken serious turn.

I also remember that Mr William B Milam, the then US Ambassador to Bangladesh had visited the flood-affected area. He was accompanied by his wife Ms Faith Henley who was generous enough to donate one tube well from her personal savings through the Rotary Club. As the president of the club, I also had an opportunity to be in their midst. When we were busily occupied in helping the affected people and also contemplating raising a donation to activate our relief and rehabilitation drive, one fine morning a young entrepreneur came down to my office and introduced himself as an expatriate entrepreneur from UK. He was none other than Mr Iqbal Ahmed for whom this account is dedicated. Mr Ahmed expressed the desire to donate seventy-five tube wells for the flood-affected people. At that point, I thought him a very dynamic and devoted person. I especially saw in him the inner desire to serve the cause of downtrodden and affected people and a willingness to contribute to the cause.

Thereafter, we joined our hands in developing a flood-affected village across the river Surma. Here, I must mention that the affluent people of Sylhet are very generous. They extended their hands to help establish an evening school, a vocational sewing training centre for the women. A few even offered their land to cultivate vegetables that were to be distributed among the poor.

To help the village to be self-sufficient to overcome the aftermath of the flood our twinning club from UK, the Rotary Club of Plymouth, joined our programme and actively participated in the reconstruction of the village by donating funds to our development projects for the villagers. We also received full support from Rotary International.

Mr Ahmed also offered support and patronisation, contributing significantly in setting up a developed Rotary village at Medini Mohol, which was inaugurated by Sir Colin Imray, the then British High Commissioner. I thus discovered him as a broad-hearted, generous person and our friendship burgeoned over the years into a permanent friendship.

In 2003 I joined Trust Bank Limited as managing director and CEO. In the meantime, Mr Ahmed, out of his desire to help the country, contributed in his own way by establishing a seafood-processing industry in Chittagong. Fortunately, he started banking with Trust Bank and routed a substantial portion of exports through us.

Ever since my early acquaintance with him, he has taken me into confidence and discussed the business plans and business-related issues with me as and when he felt to do so. As the blessings of the Almighty had it, my friend's business experienced rapid growth and expansion with his reputation and credentials both at home and abroad increasing.

Mr Ahmed has the propensity to do business with welfare orientation, something reflected in his business idea to float a budget airlines company especially aimed at helping Bangladeshi people and the diaspora to fly at cheaper fares. In 2008 he discussed the idea with me. The government had agreed in principle to consider his proposal, acknowledging it as a sincere and noble cause. As his bankers, we agreed to support this new venture and requested he prepare a project profile with a feasibility report. He arranged to conduct a feasibility report in the UK but decided not to take the venture any further due to a negative feasibility forecast which indicated that it would be a loss-making venture.

In March 2010, he invited me to a lunch meeting where he expressed the desire to set up a commercial bank to be sponsored by Non-resident Bangladeshis and to be focused inter alia on ensuring the financial welfare of the Bangladeshi diaspora who repatriate their hard-earned foreign currency. His dream came into reality when NRB Bank received its licence and was formally inaugurated by Mr Abul Maal Abdul Muhith, the finance minister, on 28 May 2013. The bank started its commercial operation with its main branch at NB Tower, Gulshan Avenue, Dhaka, inaugurated by Mr Robert W Gibson, the then British High Commissioner. At the invitation of the board of NRB Bank, I joined the institution at its very inception as advisor. Mr Ahmed had a vision to turn this institution into a bank of international standard by adopting and implementing internationally accepted good practices. At the outset, he wanted to make it a tech-savvy commercial bank by building up a sophisticated IT platform, forecasting its far-reaching positive impact on the sustainable growth of the bank.

By giving policy support on various critical important areas of operation, he has proven himself to be a man of visionary zeal with a strategic mindset. He is of the opinion that good corporate governance is a critically important factor in navigating the banking financial institution in the right direction.

IQBAL U AHMED SAYS

I had an opportunity to visit his head office and factories in Manchester, as well as other establishments, and was amazed to see what he has achieved. I feel proud of Mr Ahmed not only as my friend but also as a Bangladeshi emigrant. NRB Bank has created its own place in a very competitive market and its success on different fronts of banking operation is the result of prudent guidance and sagacity by its founder chairman.

Over the course of discussions with him on different issues on several occasions I have learned of his inherent desire to do a lot of good things for the country. He has the ingrained belief that an entrepreneur should not only be a money-spinner, but as a human being he should dedicate a good portion of his life to the cause of humanity. And that by serving the people a person can derive the heavenly pleasure which does not necessarily come from only going after money and wealth creation.

So, in NRB Bank, as a matter of policy, he focused on inclusive and sustainable growth by adopting best practices, thereby ensuring financial welfare alongside earning a profit as being the engine for growth. I wish continued success in all his present and future endeavours, and a very long, healthy and active life to my philanthropic friend.

CHAPTER TWENTY-FOUR

EDUCATION AND GIVING BACK

And then I started with education. Although computers were introduced to the world in the late 1980s and early 1990s, their arrival in Bangladesh took much longer. In my birth country, there were initially no computers in primary schools. The Bangladeshi government could not find the funding to provide them, even for secondary schools, and the government approached me for help. I had already given a computer to a school in London, which I had for a long time supported. And I had also given computers to the schools in Oldham, realising the great importance of the new technology pretty early on. So I gave money to provide many computers for schools in Bangladesh.

As I became more successful in business I was able to do much more, and I was more than happy to do so. I helped to build a mosque in Oldham, the Masjid Ul Aqsa. I was also a founder of the Islamic Centre. The community approached me, saying, 'We don't have anywhere to pray in West Oldham. We have nowhere for our children to study religion. If you can help us it would be great.' So I became involved and then suddenly I found that everybody was depending on me. 'You are God-gifted,' they say. 'You have the wealth!' I am not so sure about that but I agreed to contribute. Again, it was what I saw as fulfilling my responsibility to my community; our family provided considerable funds for the centre. I get pleasure from giving, so I was happy to do that. Local leaders used me and I was very happy to be used!

I am always on the move. And I like to get other people involved too. If I am not here who is going to run things? This is the structure I build in business or indeed in charity. I want to set everything up so that if I am not here it will still run! Whatever I have learned in my life I still see this as one of the most important principles. My executive assistant, Nita Shah, was greatly involved with my charitable activities and, as usual, she was a tower of strength and a great help.

Charity is a remarkable thing in my opinion. It crosses barriers, opens doors and provides heartwarming introductions. In Oldham, I bought a house from a gentleman called John Pellow, who used to own the Housing Units furniture store. We got to know each other very well and he asked me to join the National Health Service Trust because he was one of the trustees. John Pellow and I became very good friends and he helped to teach me a very important lesson. When he invited me to join I said. 'How much do you want? Should I write a cheque for £5,000?' He said, 'No, no, no! I don't want the money. We want your involvement because we want to encourage the majority of the Asian community, who are receiving benefits from the NHS, to become involved in the funding.' My influence was more important than my money this time, but I was very happy to give both.

I wasn't a trustee but I was already doing charity for the Trust. I was the first Asian on the Board of Trustees and we raised a lot of funds for the MRI scanner appeal for the Royal Oldham Hospital. I raised several hundred thousand pounds by involving the Asian community, and in total we raised the impressive sum of £1.2 million. We organised a huge dinner and raised many thousands of pounds and from that day a lot of Asians who used to stay away became involved in charitable work. The positive impact and the goodwill were fantastic. I am happy to claim that I was a trailblazer.

I have given a great deal of money to charity and really I feel that this work has enriched my life. It has brought me into contact with so many wonderful and inspirational people. One of the most uplifting of those is a lady called Valerie Taylor OBE. She is a British-born Bangladeshi physiotherapist who first arrived in Bangladesh with Voluntary Service Overseas in 1969. She was horrified by some of the medical conditions of some of the poorest people, particularly the desperate plight of people paralysed by spinal injury or disease and the fact that they were often left completely helpless either to beg or to die. Valerie was determined to help these people and to bring about change. She spent ten years working and campaigning and eventually in 1979 she opened the Centre for the Rehabilitation of the Paralysed, known as CRP, in Bangladesh.

Valerie began with just four patients in a disused cement warehouse but now her centre has more than 100 beds for patients. It also has a mother and child unit, a hostel, and integrated schooling for children with cerebral palsy. As well as the in-patient services offered by the centre, more than 15,000 out patients are treated every year. There is also an independent living centre for disabled women. I have raised funds for CRP and I am very proud to say that Valerie Taylor OBE has become a good friend of mine. She does wonderful work.

I have tried to help her in many ways and also introduced her to Brake Bros., a British distribution company supplying food, drink and other products, and one of my customers. Many of the British companies I deal with were delighted to help as well. I love to bring people together to do some good! I also work to raise money for the Bangladesh cancer hospitals. There are so many charities and so much work to be done.

Probably my biggest charity, or at least the one with which I have the greatest emotional bond, is the Burunga High School. I can never wipe the terrible memories I have of witnessing that dreadful massacre when I was a young boy. Previous to that event, of course, I have many happy recollections of my own time spent there. Today I am very proud that after years of association it is known as the Burunga Iqbal Ahmed High School and College. Recently the press in Bangladesh noted: 'The school has already turned into an established name in the fields of education in Sylhet. Now around 1,500 pupils are studying there. From the start this institute had been running with limited source of income and with the help of local people. Since it has added higher secondary to its activities, prominent businessman of the UK Iqbal Ahmed OBE got involved with its managing board and has been providing financial help generously so that the standard of teaching has been greatly improved.'

My support for my old school began many years ago when one of my old teachers, Mr Massabir Ali, came to see me. He said, 'Oh, we heard about your success, and we are all very pleased that you are doing so well. We are very proud that you were a student of the school, and because you were my student and I was your teacher I feel particularly proud.'

It was very good to see him again after so many years, but there was a sadness about him and I soon learned why. He said, 'I would like to take you to our school and show you what it looks like now, but you would not like it. The place is falling apart, and so are the standards of education for the children.' He seemed very downhearted and upset. Of course I had to investigate for myself and I very quickly discovered that he was absolutely right: Burunga High School was in real trouble.

I knew I would help them from that moment, but I didn't want to rush in waving a chequebook and playing the big hero. That is not my way. I like to start slowly and carefully. First, I wanted to offer them a computer. I gave them that in the early 1990s. A computer seems a small thing, but I had seen technology improve so much in my lifetime. In my day we were not allowed a ballpoint pen in school; it had to be a fountain pen. Electronic calculators were not allowed in the school. The rule was you had to do all the maths calculations yourself.

When I started the business we still had telex machines. Sending a telex was a nightmare; we used to sit for hours and hours on the telex machines sending messages. Then there was a fax machine. It took us six months to trust that machine, and I never did understand how it works! Then the computer arrived and we thought, 'Wow! We are 100 years ahead.' It was a magical move forward that would transform the world.

That was why I thought the best donation initially I could make to the school was a computer. It could help with so much of the work of running the school. I was a real computer enthusiast. I had bought computers for all my kids, my brothers, and everyone in the family. They are fantastic. I also gave a few to Oldham School and to a school in Camden, London, where an old friend was a contact. At the time a computer was my regular first reaction. If somebody wanted some help, I gave them a computer. In fact I still give computers, especially to my school. Every two or three years when we replace all our worktops at Seamark, everything is recycled and sent to the school in Bangladesh everyone enjoys it.

After that, when they came to me they said they wanted to build an auditorium because numbers at the school had increased so much that they couldn't have everyone together. I sympathised because I could see they were victims of their own success. I asked my only cousin Shanoor, who was previously a student there and who takes care of our interests in Sylhet, to pay and help them. So an auditorium was built. Once we had done that they wanted me to buy some land so they could have a field and play cricket on it. I bought the field and spent quite a lot of money preparing the land so the children could play football and cricket safely. This was all fine. I was pleased to assist because of course I feel a special bond with the school.

But the demands never stopped. Next they wanted something else, and a string of requests followed. They were all for relatively small things, and I did not ever like to say no. In the end they said, 'Can you build a new school building? Can you finance us to build a building?' This was a lot of money. I was a little uncertain for a time. Slowly and gradually, people kept coming to my house asking and the pressure built up. 'You can do it,' they said. After a while I knew there was no alternative. I had to agree to help out in a big way. I wanted to do what they were asking. I knew it was the right thing to do. And so I said, 'OK.'

They offered to name the school after me, something I considered a huge honour. There are many examples in Bangladesh of colleges and institutions under the names of people who have contributed greatly. I was proud to join them. I was a little shy at first, but they insisted they really wanted to put my own name to it because I had done so much. 'If you can do this it will be great,' they said. 'We can show you are the most successful man in the world from Bangladesh.' I felt happy that they wanted to share this with the world, so I said, 'Go for it!' I think my story inspires the children who are there now, which is why I am so passionately involved it. The transformation is amazing. There were only 300 to 400 pupils and now there are 1,500 and every year they produce good results. It is fantastic.

It took quite a time to arrange everything, a couple of years at least. One of my conditions was that I would agree to give them the money, and with their terms and conditions, but, I said, 'I want to build a college alongside the school there.' At first they did not accept this suggestion. 'Oh this is too difficult,' they said. 'Where are you going to get the principals and teachers.' I insisted that the college had to run parallel with the school and had to be managed by the same committee. Then I would provide the funds. I couldn't convince them at first. It took quite a long time because they couldn't seem to accept the idea of having a college in that area. I think because it is such a rural area. I talked to Shanoor and told him to convince them and make them understand that the existing college was too far from the school. They eventually agreed after some persuasion from him.

But I had not finished with my conditions. I also wanted it to be a college for girls as well as boys. Traditionally in Bangladesh, girls drop out of school much too early and start doing household chores or getting married young. It was compulsory for both boys and girls go to school, but sometimes the girls didn't go. Sometimes their parents don't allow them to. I said, 'Look I firmly believe in full education for females because I have seen my grandmother and my mother and they are so impressive.' If you educate one woman in a house you don't need to worry about their generation. That's it. One educated woman will produce educated children and an educated generation. Before then the boys left school at fifteen or sixteen and the girls often very much earlier. I felt at least if they had a college, both boys and girls would have a better chance of achieving in life. There are so many factors here. I tried to explain that times are changing: 'Number one nowadays is the ability to earn a living and that is important for both boys and girls. Even if a girl gets married she still wants to earn money in life.' That's why jobs in communication and technology are so important, which is why I sent a computer.

We have to be liberal and open and cater for all children,' I said. 'This is my vision. If a girl is educated, an educated boy will marry her because she can be very productive. She can get a job; she can look smart. The second thing is that she can easily get a job working for a council, NGO government departments, a manufacturing company or even as a schoolteacher.' I believe the favourite teacher is the best teacher. They can inspire pupils to do everything from building business to becoming better home economists.

I simply gave them myself as an example. I am from this village and I have become a successful businessman. I brought a lot of successful British people like Rushanara Ali MP, who was born in the village close by, and Anwar Chowdhury, the British High Commissioner to Bangladesh at the time to visit the school. This man was also born in a village very close to ours and he has become a top civil servant. Then I brought Baroness Sayeeda Warsi. She was very impressive; I could see the eyes of some of our children opening wide in amazement at her achievements. Sayeeda Warsi said to the children, 'We are no different from you. I come from Pakistan but I managed to become chairman of the Conservative Party in the UK.' It was so inspiring. I was so proud that I had created this college and given these pupils these amazing chances in life. You can get there,' I said to them. These are some of the influences and encouragement I have given.

The school in Burunga gives me immense pleasure. I really love to see all those children I am helping. I am so proud that we have transformed it from it being rundown and performing poorly into a well-equipped, properly staffed and highly efficient institution. It had not been easy as during those times when I was busy making sure that everything was satisfactory – the buildings, the field, the furniture, the classrooms, as well as motivating the children and their parents to aim for better results – a group of left-wing politicians was campaigning against me. They were saying that I had a motive for doing all this work and that I was after a nomination as MP. Of course this was not true. They realised later on that I was there only to help and the matter died down.

You would not believe how many thousands of people from that school are studying in universities all over the world. When Rushanara Ali visited the school, her PA, Sadiq Islam, said while we were travelling from the city to the school, 'I am looking forward to seeing your school.' I replied, 'That is nice to hear, me too!' He then said, 'My mother studied in your school and it was a wonderful experience for her.' I could not believe what I was hearing. I already felt proud of what we had achieved and here was the son of a former student who studied at my school. Suddenly I felt extra proud!

Then came the problems with the parents. Once I had delivered the school, the parents wanted help. They were asking for all kinds of help. I started dealing directly with the students. I said: 'If you want to be somebody, if you want a bright future, if you don't want to be a labourer and go to the Middle East and work on a building site, living on the roadside, then you need an education. If you get a good education you don't need to go anywhere. You can stay in Bangladesh and get a good job.' I always tell the students that when I invested in this school I was expecting a return. 'I want good results from you. That is all I want,' I told them. This is why the school is getting the best results in the country.

There are 70 per cent girls in my school and they are so smart. They can speak English in the village; you couldn't even think of people doing that when I was young. They do everything so well, they have earned themselves their very bright future.

The education they receive makes a huge difference to their lives. They can do anything with a good education. This I believe is the best kind of charity.

CHAPTER TWENTY-FIVE

PUBLIC WORK AND CHARITY

The responsibility to help others is something that is always with me, and often I find it more helpful to others if I give my time rather than my money. One of the most interesting types of charity work I like to be involved in is being a consultant. I feel a great part of my overall contribution to society has involved being an adviser to many government bodies.

The first time I was invited to help was by DTI Minister Tony Baldry in the late 1990s. He invited me to join the Southern Asian Advisory Group on outward investment. SAAG, as it was known, had the responsibility to promote British businesses into Southern Asian countries for inward and outward investments. I was one of several advisers, part of the delegation for South Asia, several times organising seminars and networking. It was a very good experience. I felt it was good to be asked and the experience helped me to learn so much about how I could contribute to British society. Even as a boy from a remote Bangladeshi village who arrived in this country with very little, I never felt inferior to being thrust into encounters with the great and the good of this country. I am open and honest and if I do not understand something I am not afraid to ask. Happily, it was an uplifting time because even among some of the important people of the land I felt as if I was one of them. I was treated very well, I am happy to say, and I believe my experience was helpful.

I was an adviser for about three years. Ian Dale OBE was the chairman and after a time he also became the chairman of BOND, which was a part of the British Council that provided finance for the training and education of civil servants to help enhance their performance. It was all to do with helping to foster a sense of 'Britishness', and the British ambassadors to the Commonwealth countries and their civil servants were also involved. High-quality professionals are selected overseas and assigned to UK companies for up to twelve months. Seamark was a participant in the scheme and I was asked to be an adviser. When I went there I thought I was invited to be a member of this board to help encourage the British Council because I am Bangladeshi. Some of my skilled and highly trained relatives had been involved in that project a long time before and they had a great experience. Long afterwards they used to talk about how wonderful the British Council was to them.

The first day in the UK, when we were all doing the introductions, I remember everybody chatting to each other for the first time. I was not at all sure how to proceed, but I took a deep breath and I just said, 'I am Iqbal Ahmed. I am from Bangladesh and I run a business and I am so honoured to be here to help. If there is anything I can do to help my country, it would be a great privilege.' There was a sort of embarrassed pause. The director was looking at the chairman and the chairman was looking at the director. 'Is there anything wrong?' I said. 'Iqbal,' said the chairman Ian Dale, 'I don't think you have been very well briefed. You are not representing Bangladesh. You are representing Great Britain.' There was much laughter. I apologised for my ignorance, but it didn't matter. I cannot deny my background and I was delighted for them to make use of me. These are the things you enjoy, and you learn from your mistakes. And also, of course, it underlined my acceptance in this wonderful country. I am proud to have been born a Bangladeshi and I am also proud to live my life as a Briton.

I was there as an adviser for BOND for quite a few years and then after the Labour Party won the election and the Tony Blair government came to power in 1997 it became part of the Department of Trade and Industry. Stephen Byers was the Minister for the DTI and he invited me to join his advisory board, which was called the Competitiveness Council. At these meetings, a lot of discussion took place. Digby Jones was the chairman of the CBI; there was a professor from Oxford, the chief executive of Marks and Spencer, and a consultant from PricewaterhouseCoopers. I faced a table full of top people and here I was: Iqbal Ahmed, a young man who sold a lot of prawns but did not have much talking power! Facing a learned professor and famous people like Digby Jones, I was a bit worried about what I was going to say, how they would accept me. The first day I took Stephen Byers to one side and I said, 'Look Stephen, I think you have picked the wrong man here. It is not that I don't want to be here, but I think these people can speak much better than I can. I don't think you'll see me at the next board meeting.'

He said, 'Oh, no, no, no, Iqbal! You are exactly the man we need in this group. We thought about it and we decided you were the founder of a great business and you were the challenger who took on much adversity to succeed. These people are talking because they get paid for talking. They are clever and articulate certainly, but you are the real man. It is you we want to hear from. Your drive and experience sets you apart from all of the rest of us. You must stay in the group. We will be so much worse off without you'!

I had to think about it for a while, but this was quite an accolade. I was quite moved, to be honest. I decided that Stephen Byers was a wise and impressive man. He put his hand on my shoulder and insisted I must stay. After what he had said I could hardly walk out, although I still had my reservations. There were quite a few fascinating items on the agenda over the years and one was: 'How to create an entrepreneur in British society,' a meeting I went along to four weeks later.

Some people said we should create a textbook to help our teachers; others that we should send our teachers to Silicon Valley and create systems in our textbooks or curriculums, and there should be a system. Everybody was talking and nobody came to a decision. I am still undecided about whether you can learn to be an entrepreneur from a textbook. Since then I have studied a little bit more, read books from Harvard University and Stanford about entrepreneurism, and I am still not sure how much any would-be entrepreneur needs teaching. He or she needs to be willing to learn, certainly, and keen to pick up ideas from wherever they are, but much more has to come from within than without, I believe.

Then I was under pressure to talk at the following board meeting. Before the break I didn't say much; I was quite nervous and a lot of ideas were discussed. Stephen Byers told us all before the board meeting that if the division bell rang he would leave and not say anything. 'My secretary will take the telephone call with the message about a vote in the House and I will have to go,' he said. 'There is a tunnel from my office to Parliament. I am afraid you will have to excuse me.' I thought, 'If he leaves I hope he comes back very soon.' He left and I was without his friendly support among these great brains.

For a while I was nervous as the vote took place in Parliament, but he came back. We talked and he did a great deal to restore my confidence. 'So,' he said, 'you will be absolutely fine. Just be yourself and give us the benefit of your hands-on experience.' Eventually he just looked at me and said, 'Let us hear from Iqbal Ahmed, the successful entrepreneur.'

'Look, I'm not used to this kind of board,' I started. 'There are a lot of important people here. It is nice to be here and I am learning a lot, but it is by no means my kind of arena. But there is one thing I would like to share about my success. I have done well so far, but I am not yet fully successful. I still have quite a way to go and quite a lot left to achieve. But I like to feel proud of whatever I have done in my life up to date and I would like to express my gratitude for the many people who have helped me along the way.'

I continued, 'There used to be an organisation called Business Link and they were the people who gave advice on how to run a business. I had all sorts of help from the government in different schemes and it was great. I had this opportunity because I was keen and I had some friends to hold my hand. I feel like I have got a flavour of entrepreneurism. I feel like that if a person like me, Iqbal Ahmed, maybe ten years ago could get help the way I got help, there are thousands of people who could be an entrepreneur with the level of help that exists now, and without a textbook.

'For example, the man or woman who is running a small trading or manufacturing company or other small or medium business can succeed and grow if they get real support and good advice that provides the incentive to create jobs. Probably one day some of the small businessmen and women of our country will become entrepreneurs and this can happen immediately because they're already on the way. But I believe the drive and the initiative has to come from within.'

Everybody was silent. I couldn't tell what they were thinking. Some of them were looking at my eyes and some were looking down at the floor. What I said came from my experience because I saw my future as bright, and I knew that for those people on the street, running petrol pumps or a corner shop, who were often struggling, it would brighten their lives to simply give them some helpful advice. A big discussion started following that meeting, and the initiative that became known as the New Deal was created from that conversation. It happened without my knowledge because I was so busy, but I found out the blueprint came after the meeting I'd spoken at. The New Deal was created and it helped many people. That's something I like to think I made a contribution to. I encourage anybody who wants to get on and succeed in any field to get advice from people who know what they are talking about.

Later I was involved in many other projects. Food Industry Sustainability Strategy (FISS) looked at how to create a sustainable volume of organic food for generations to come. As with many other initiatives, on my part this was purely voluntary work, where I was happy to share my experience free of charge. I am more than happy to do this. I still take on many tasks like this; it means I can then become a catalyst for things to really happen, which I love. I have been invited to become a business catalyst for British groups all over the world, so whenever I speak, naturally I share my enthusiasm for British export promotion. I enjoy it very much and I am still working with the community, too.

Then I thought, why not introduce the same scheme to my own community? Now a few of the most successful people who have businesses in Bangladesh and in Britain have got together. Two years ago we created a project called the UK and Bangladesh Catalysts of Commerce and Industry. UKBCCI is a leading umbrella organisation for successful British-Bangladeshi entrepreneurs in the UK and Bangladesh to promote British and Bangladeshi products. Our aim is to bring together these leading businesses by networking with them and setting up links, programmes and projects that not only build up confidence in the UKBCCI, but also connect with them both in the UK and Bangladesh. We are determined to establish and create the next generation of entrepreneurs and business leaders for the future.

We want people to invest in both Great Britain and in Bangladesh and transfer knowledge and trade that can help both countries. A businessman like me can make a difference if I can create jobs in Bangladesh and bring revenue back to Britain. This creates wealth for both countries by building bridges. We are very selective with our members and directors but we are full of excellent plans and ideas. We are like a think

191

tank. This is where I can talk to Bangladeshi students and transfer knowledge. We study both countries in-depth and how the relationship can benefit both.

I didn't have a higher education, leaving school at just fifteen years old, but I still see the enormous benefits of good teaching. Maybe a person like me is different; I feel that I am exceptional. I see a lot of bright children and educated children and they are struggling. They have got education but not so much ambition. Education is important, but my own personal view is that you have to have ambition as well. I had the vision from my childhood and because I had that vision I learned as I went on. It was the driving force in my life. I took some time to find the right business for me, but once I found it I did not deviate. From being a small boy I had great ambition. I was not a good scholar at school but I was always anxious to learn what I wanted to learn. Having that ambition driving me on, I educated myself in the ways of the world.

There are parallels between education and ambition but they are quite different things. Many people feel education is helpful to your ambitions, so you can plan ahead much more easily, and perhaps that is true for some of us. But other people are a little different. They are focused on success and nothing is going to get in their way. Their education, or lack of it, is not a major factor in their life. I hold my hand up and say I am a person like that. Steve Jobs, who created the success that is Apple, or Bill Gates of Microsoft, were driven men with a passion for what they were doing and where they were going. They had a vision. They had something special and they worked very, very hard. A formal education does not always guarantee success.

When I started, with my Transit van, I used to work a minimum of twelve to fifteen hours a day, which was exceptional. I would not ask my son to work the way I worked because my life was very different. It was a tough life. I have experienced my family fleeing their country and leaving behind their wonderful property. I have seen the war and the death and destruction it brings. I have seen the racism. I have seen all of the worst sides of life. In my life I have I believe faced all the worst things. And I have overcome them.

I love the way charity work helps to bridge the gaps between different races. It is the best way to bring people together. I see it very much as a sort of wonderful by-product of everything I have done. It's brilliant. I think every human has the responsibility to do some sort of charity work. In my book, you can't be successful and hold your head up without helping a charity. You can't become popular without it. You can't become a good politician without giving. Charity is vital in life and every child should be taught its importance from the very early years. I find it very hard to say no, but these days I receive so many requests that I have to say no sometimes.

I was approached by the The Prince's Seeing is Believing programme, a Business in the Community initiative, to become involved. And I was of course delighted to accept. I participated as part of a delegation that visited some schools in deprived areas in Manchester and London and we reported back to HRH The Prince of Wales.

I was also invited to join Mosaic, also founded by HRH The Prince of Wales, in 2007. Mosaic's mission is to create opportunities for young people of all backgrounds growing up in deprived areas, to inspire them to realise their talents and potential. Mosaic's mentoring programs in schools and prisons are delivered by volunteers and aimed at lifting the aspirations of young people and closing the gap between those aspirations and their attainment. One of the Prince's passions is for the power of positive thinking and this plays a major part in the organisation's ethos.

I go and I talk to anybody who will listen because this is a wonderful cause. My example works. I always like to speak about my school in Burunga as I am very proud of what we have achieved there, but I am happy to answer questions on anything I have done. I like to have people follow me – or do better.

CHAPTER TWENTY-SIX

PRINCE CHARLES

I have been extremely lucky to have received the support of the Royal Family throughout my career. Not only have I been to HM The Queen's garden party at Buckingham Palace, I have also been inside the Palace for my investiture, receiving the OBE from Prince Charles. Of course, I also had the good fortune to meet HRH Princess Anne when she inaugurated my factory in Bangladesh.

I have been lucky enough to meet Prince Charles a few times. The first time was in 1995 when he visited our stand during the IFE (International Food and Drink Exhibition) in Earls Court, London. Seamark was member of the British Frozen Food Federation and its director general at the time was Alf Carr, a good friend of mine. He was with the Federation for quite a long time. He called me in advance to tell me that Prince Charles would be visiting our stand. We were launching our brands, Mr Prawn and Tiger Brand, produced from our first factory in Openshaw, Manchester, and it was perfect timing. Myself, Bilal and Nita were at the show.

It was such a pleasant encounter. Prince Charles asked many questions. Where are the products from? Where do we sell? He showed genuine interest in our products. He also mentioned that if Seamark were to be successful in exporting, we should apply for the Queen's Award For Export, which we did, winning the Queen's Award for Export Achievement in 1998. I also had another opportunity to meet Prince Charles in early 2000 when I attended a reception in Kensington Palace as part of a delegation of Business in the Community's Seeing is Believing Program.

CHAPTER TWENTY-SEVEN

MY BANK

I travelled to Bangladesh several times a year with trade delegates when I was an adviser to SAAG (Southern Asia Advisory Group) under the DTI. I also represented other organisations. During these times I met some influential people from both the public and private sectors. I also saw the potential of investing in Bangladesh as I felt it was my responsibility to encourage British investment in various industries in the country.

What I saw and learned during these visits greatly interested me and I decided to establish my own company's production and processing facilities in Bangladesh. I asked my then financial controller, Alec Dodgeon, who I spoke about earlier, to accompany me to Bangladesh. He and I did a lot of research and gathered information from different government departments, including the Prime Minister's office and the Board of Investment (BOI). I remember Mr Farooq Sobhan was then the BOI chairman with ministerial status. Alec and I were encouraged and given the support by the British High Commission to make a British investment in Chittagong. We invested and set up the business, the company that is Seamark BD Limited. It has been running successfully since the year 2000, exporting all kinds of seafood, but mainly tiger shrimps. We have expanded since then and earned a huge reputation over the years, receiving many gold medals and trophies from the Bangladeshi Prime Minister in recognition of the company's high exports.

As the economy began to strengthen, and the country's GDP became more stable, the rise in foreign investment made Bangladesh more attractive, especially in the textiles and readymade garments industry.

Creating a financial institution is a discussion that I had been a part of on a few occasions, but at first nothing materialised. It was simply discussions and exchanges of opinions among friends and business associates.

In late 2009, I attended a dinner that was held in Dhaka for a group of medical doctors from the UK. Some of the guests in attendance were my friends, so I was looking forward to the dinner. When I arrived I found myself sitting with a group of people I did not know very well. After dinner, while mingling with the guests, I spotted my friend the British High Commissioner to Bangladesh, Stephen Evans OBE. When I served as the chairman of the chamber of commerce, we worked together on several occasions at various seminars and networking events. Stephen had visited our factories in Bangladesh and offices in Manchester, and was fully aware of the extent of our operations. While at this dinner we were mainly discussing the importance of British inward investment into the country and the importance of our ongoing contributions to Bangladesh.

The Bangladesh finance minister, Mr Abul Maal Abdul Muhith, was also in attendance on that occasion and was seated not far from Stephen and myself. Mr Muhith hails from Sylhet and is also the MP for Sylhet. The region is quite famous for producing finance ministers: two previous finance ministers, namely Mr Saifur Rahman and Mr Shah AMS Kibria, were from the same region.

Stephen became very anxious and said, 'Do you know the finance minister?' I said, 'Yes, he is my MP and he is from my home town'. Stephen asked, 'Why is he not talking to you?' Suddenly he grabbed my hand and led me to the minister to make the introduction: 'Minister, do you know Iqbal Ahmed? He is the most successful British investor in Bangladesh. You must visit his factory, thousands of people work for him.' The finance minister Mr Muhith smiled and responded while holding my hand: 'Iqbal is a rare breed of our country and also from my constituency, so I can say I know him very well.' While the minister and I spoke, it became apparent to Stephen that we knew each other quite well.

The finance minister then invited me to his office. Following that meeting I met with him a few times and approached him about the possibility of establishing a financial institution targeted at Non-resident Bangladeshis (NRBs). He immediately showed an interest, saying it was a marvellous proposal and would be welcomed by many NRBs living all over the world. He suggested that if I could bring together the many successful NRBs living in various different countries and give them the possibility of investing in Bangladesh, it would be highly beneficial both for the economy of Bangladesh and for the diaspora. Bangladesh would earn more foreign currency and create economic ambassadors out of all the investors.

It was a huge surprise and quite a challenge; however, I could see the benefit to Bangladesh. I was extremely flattered by the minister's recommendation and felt enthused by the challenge, but I could see that there was potential for trouble and a high level of complexity. This would not be an easy task.

With more than a few misgivings, I decided to take on this daunting and difficult job. It was anything but simple. Those who have set up banks are certainly brave and patient people. There were many, many meetings, one after the other, and progress at times was painfully slow. Sometimes I felt out of my depth and thought, 'Doing a bank. . . how am I going to do a bank?' You have to be well prepared and knowledgeable about finance and economics, and so I studied everything I could on the subject. I attended many financial seminars and also a training course on international finance.

Although this was a new sector, it has always been a keen interest of mine. I often questioned why I had taken the job and it was because of my love for Bangladesh. I can see so much potential in my country and the minister's plan made good sense.

Mr Muhith was very passionate about his support for the idea. I gave him a name: Non-Resident Bangladeshi Bank. It soon became shortened to NRB bank, with the tagline: Not Just Another Bank. The minister wanted all the investment in the new bank to come from NRB Diaspora living abroad to benefit the country with much-needed foreign currency capital. The idea is that money comes into Bangladesh from people working abroad, who send their remittances through this new bank.

Soon I began to share the vision of the minister for creating such a financial institution. I began to dream of unlocking a new horizon to the Bangladesh economy by facilitating NRB inward investment in Bangladesh and assisting Bangladeshi enterprises to access international markets.

The meeting with the minister Mr Muhith took place more than five years ago and it took me two and a half years to find all the investors from different countries. There are an abundance of successful Bangladeshis all over the world and I travelled thousands of miles to find them. It didn't bother me, because by then I was on a mission, and grew to be more passionate about the project than the minister. It was something I wanted to do for the Non-resident Bangladeshi people, a project that would allow them to develop a crucially important link with their home country. I was running round all over the world, persuading and convincing people to lend their support and their money to the NRB Bank. I visited and held numerous meetings with the relevant government high officials.

In 2013, I set up the bank and I am pleased to say that it has become very successful. However, I would have not achieved this without the help and support of many people. I must also send my appreciation to the government of Bangladesh and the Honourable Prime Minister Sheikh Hasina, the Ministry of Finance and the Central Bank of Bangladesh for giving me and other Non-resident Bangladeshis the opportunity to set up financial institutions for NRBs in Bangladesh.

As well as the founder, I have been the chairman of the board of NRB Bank for the past three years. I have found this to be one of the most honourable things I have achieved for my country of birth, which I love deeply.

It was certainly not an easy task. I had trouble finding investors from some parts of the world, such as the UK and USA and the Middle East. However, we were able to gather investors from Japan, Singapore, Malaysia, the Philippines, Italy and others. Successful people are very often busy people and sometimes they do no not want to be tracked down. Not many were interested in Bangladesh at the first approach and persuading them needed frequent meetings. Fortunately, I managed to convince enough people at the last minute and fulfil the investment obligation.

We have a board of twenty directors, which is the maximum number. I travel to Bangladesh every month to conduct the board meetings. And we have forty-six shareholders. They are entrepreneur investors from all over the world. After a three-year lock-in period we can sell our shares to the public, which would be one of the biggest tasks. It took me a lot of time, effort and energy to build the success of NRB bank, but I'm pleased to say we have already opened many branches all over Bangladesh and continue to do so.

NRB Bank has provided hundreds of jobs and financed many businesses. Three years ago we were given some guidelines from the Bangladesh Central Bank. Now that first meeting seems a long time ago, because so much effort and energy has gone into NRB Bank since. I see its creation as another successful chapter in my career.

CHAPTER TWENTY-EIGHT

SUCCESS AGAIN

Today my company Seamark is huge and successful. I am chairman and chief executive of the Seamark Group of Companies which, for the record, comprises Seamark PLC, Seamark (BD) Ltd., Seamark Holdings Ltd., Seamark USA Inc., IBCO Ltd., IBCO Enterprise, IBCO Food Industries Ltd., IBCO (BD) Ltd., Restaurant Wholesale, Vermilion Restaurant, and Openshaw Holdings Ltd. Seamark Group employs more than 4,000 people worldwide.

A lot of British seafood companies started around the same time, in the early 90s. Many of them are non-existent now because most of the business went to the Far East and Southern Asia. But because we worked unbelievably hard and because we have a link with Bangladesh and other parts of Asia, we managed to survive and we did well. Some say we have been lucky but we say, like many a famous sportsman, the harder we work the luckier we get! Our business is very seasonal and very competitive. Like many successful business, we thrive on competition.

Another success came in the form of Vermilion. In 1999, we acquired a six-and-a-half-acre site in Manchester but as the 2002 Commonwealth Games were being held only half a mile away at the Manchester City stadium, the council decided to keep the land for parking as a condition. Construction began in 2003 with the foundation laid by myself and George Osborne, the MP for Tatton in Cheshire, and later to be Chancellor of the Exchequer. The project included one of the largest cold-storage facilities in the North-West, a wholesale trade counter, offices and a building with infrastructure for a restaurant.

In 2005, the government announced the creation of an expert panel to decide on the location of a super casino and sixteen smaller casinos. This casino was a £260m investment, which Manchester won in 2007, against Blackpool and London's Millennium Dome. It would create 2,700 jobs.

I pursued the idea of a restaurant, as there would be a chance that the super casino would be built close by. However, the scheme was rejected in February 2008.

Vermilion was one of the boldest projects to hit the landscape in Manchester. I decided to create a restaurant that was very different to any other in Manchester or in most major cities. A restaurant that oozed luxury and opulence, with an Asian fusion influence and atmosphere, something Manchester had never seen before.

Renowned in his field, Miguel Cancio Martins, the designer of Buddha-Bar Paris and Man Ray in the same city, as well as the Alain Ducasse Crystal restaurant within the Pacha nightclub in Marrakech, was appointed as the interior designer for the space.

We also appointed kitchen consultant Ken Winch, who designed the kitchens of Buckingham Palace, Hakkasan and Windsor Castle. We also took on Jonathan Bolcover as architect for the project, as well as quantity surveyor Simon Fenton. Our hugely successful launch night took place in November 2007.

In the meantime, through Seamark's seafood supply connection and longtime friends in Thailand, Poj and Vichittra Aramwatananont, we appointed Chumpol Jangprai as head chef; he also held a weekly Thai cooking school. Again through Miguel, we appointed Dominique Gelin, previously manager at Buddha-Bar Paris, to run the restaurant. The restaurant was named Vermilion, as it best described the venue's colour scheme.

The huge three-storey restaurant and bar stands majestically in Sport City, Manchester, which includes landmarks such as the Manchester City Stadium and concert venue, as well as Thomas Heatherwick's iconic sculpture *B of the Bang*, although that has now been removed.

The £5 million project included a 200-capacity Thai fusion restaurant, a cocktail bar with a capacity of 300, a large private dining room and a function room. It features unusual spectacles such as a Buddha tower and cocoons. However, the most fundamental aspect of the venue was, and remains, its style, different to anything else in Manchester. It has its own bar (Cinnabar) within the premises, with DJs playing while you eat, very dimmed lighting, detailed designs from thirty-six different countries, and large and opulent spaces. It brought the atmosphere of a major city venue to Manchester.

Even though the super casino scheme was rejected in 2008, Vermilion has continued to thrive due to the longevity of its design, atmosphere and style. To this day it still stands out as the most luxuriously designed restaurant in Manchester.

Since the launch , many articles about the restaurant have appeared in the media, including *Marie Claire*, the *Manchester Evening News*, *Business Traveller*, *ShortList*, *Cosmopolitan*, the BBC, *Cheshire Life*, *GQ*, *Glamour*, *Class*, *BMW Magazine*, *Arena*, *Wallpaper*, and *Olive*.

Celebrities who have visited Vermilion include Hollywood film director Tim Burton, former Prime Minister David Cameron, players from both Manchester United and Manchester City, England's cricket team, The Script, Ricky Hatton (and 1,500 guests), various footballers' wives, and stars from *Coronation Street* and *Hollyoaks*. Vermilion is also regularly used as a location for various TV shows, music videos and photo shoots.

We have hosted art events such as VOX art gallery with curators International 3. And in 2016, nine years after its launch, Vermilion will open its 1,000-capacity banquet hall, behind the restaurant.

Out of all the businesses I have created in my life, Vermilion has been the most exciting project. It gives me an unlimited level of joy and satisfaction to see the restaurant filled with friends and family dining together, celebrating special occasions, and enjoying the food and atmosphere.

Although Vermilion is not an easy task, my son Manzur rises to the challenge every day. From the start of construction up until today, he has been there examining every detail, making sure that every aspect of the restaurant, from the food to the service, is kept to an impeccable standard.

The 'million prawns a minute' claim is still true. In fact the exact figure, of course, depends on the size of the prawns – if you have more small ones you do more! We are not just about prawns. We have expanded to include many items. It is not always wise to focus on a single product in this business. We have found it is always better to have a range of products to rely upon. To be flexible I can always alternate productions with different products. We do all kinds of seafood and lots of dry products and spices, and many other frozen products.

When I was starting I couldn't have imagined I would succeed to this degree. I knew that I would start a business of some sort in my life. Whether I would become a contractor, a builder or some kind of engineering enterprise, or have a business in textiles, I did not know, but to run a business was always my intention. I never saw any other way of becoming successful and I still don't. I am a difficult person to work for, certainly. I am demanding because I want the business to do well. But I am fair and I always reward people who work hard for me very well. Although I have had to make many difficult decisions in the UK and Bangladesh, I have never lost any of my faithful staff.

If you work for somebody else there are so many hurdles to get over. Even to get a job can be a nightmare task. Where I was brought up In Bangladesh you have to have an uncle, or some other convenient relative, to recommend you for a nice safe job with the government. In the UK, you have a tough time because although the system is perhaps fairer, you have to start from the floor. Even if you become a successful doctor or dentist it is very hard and involves many years of intense studying. But to become a successful businessman is simple as long as you get your head in the right place, you motivate yourself and stay focused.

The further you can take your business the more money you can make! You buy from the source and sell to the buyer, and the further you can increase the differences between what you buy for and what you sell for, the more money you make, the more people you can employ, and the more jobs you can create. If you get it right, your profits start increasing. Sometimes you can buy and sell in the same place and still make money. It is all about your relationship with the source and the buyer.

How soon after getting the Transit van and first starting trading did I realise it was going to work? That is a question people so often ask me. And the answer is that I knew straight away. I was always good at maths. At school I might not have worked particularly hard very often, but my maths was always first class. I had this God-given gift. I was going to work hard whether I made money or not. It doesn't take me a long time to make a decision; it is something that is in me. I can make decisions very quickly and I am always surprised that so many other people cannot. I know the answers straight away – whether it is going to work or it is not going to work. Once you have made the correct decision it is up to you. If you can't make it work there must be something wrong. You are not working hard. The chemistry is not right.

CHAPTER TWENTY-NINE

WHO I AM NOW

The importance of family is a constant theme all the way through my life. I always put family first. I believe children, family and friends come before anything, and I make a lot of sacrifices for my friends, regardless of their wealth.

Sometimes I think I will retire one day; I don't think I will go on and on forever. For the time when I will not be here, I am trying to set up ways for things to continue. I am already releasing control, my family is gradually taking more responsibility. All my companies are run by the management and they are members of a team. In the future, I think I will spend more time on my charity work and maybe reduce my hours, but I enjoy the business very much.

I do play golf and tennis – I have a very painful tennis elbow – but I should play more to keep myself fit. I would like to spend more time with my family and enjoy life as I have worked very hard from an early age. I want to see my son build a family, my future generation. He is a gentleman and I want to see him have kids. I enjoy spending time with my grandchildren, and taking more holidays. But I would not lie on a beach and do nothing – that's not Iqbal! Nowadays, I enjoy reading books, travelling and talking and sharing my knowledge and experience. After all, I have packed in a great deal and had a fascinating journey. I am not somebody who was born with a silver spoon in his mouth. I want my company to do well and my family to be happy. I look forward to the day when everything can run trouble-free without me.

I think the race situation has improved here. Because I was here during that time when everybody was worried that foreign people like me coming to take their jobs and their homes, I could understand the fear and the bad feeling. Now I think most people understand that immigration is here to stay and it is a positive thing for our country. We all like to see everyone in their own way contributing to society. As long as people don't take each other's share we can all be happy. Whoever is living anywhere, as long as you contribute to the society you are living in, and living a good life without harming anyone else, I think you can be accepted anywhere in the world. I think it is fantastic when you are accepted.

I won't be going into politics. I have been asked (see later in this chapter), but that is not me. I don't think I would make a good politician. I could probably run an NGO and do a lot of social work, and this is what I will do; part of my job will always be charitable, creating entrepreneurs, raising money for good causes. I have many people asking me for advice and I am generous with my time. I like to talk with young people and learn from them and give them some flavour of what I have gone through in my life.

When I was younger I thought you should not become too ambitious. You cannot think one day I'll own an airline or build the tallest building in the city. You can't think like this because you have to build trust within your own communities first. There are certain things you can't do. But gradually I have done everything I could have imagined and proved myself wrong! For the last twenty-five years or so, from the 1990s, I have felt much more comfortable here than in the country where I was born, in fact more than anywhere else in the world. It happened as soon as I realised that my voice is heard and is acceptable and that if I say something I am respected, and not discriminated against. When I speak at the Round Table or when I start talking as an adviser for the South Asian Advisory Board for the DTI, I realise that even as a brown-skinned man I am part of the group.

I think I became very strong when my father left us and I had to go through the Liberation War in Bangladesh. Although I was young I had to become the head of the family. I came here to a completely different environment and it was a challenge that I had to face up to. When I then went to London for six years that was an even bigger challenge, and then when I returned to Oldham to help my family business when my father was sick, I could see nothing but debts! Then I took charge of my brothers one after the other when my father and mother left to go back to Bangladesh.

I couldn't stop looking ahead. I couldn't stop being ambitious. I wanted more and more. Everywhere in my early years there was a shortage of cash, always. I had good people around me and I never stopped. Since I started writing cheques – and this is what I feel proud of – I have honoured every cheque; I have never cheated anybody and my word is my bond. I have signed millions of cheques and never once has a single cheque been dishonoured. I could have had ambitions to become even richer, but I did not do that because I struggled with that.

I am not like any other Englishman who was brought up here and has all the support and advantages he needed. I had to struggle and I had to fight for things. I only see the dream of what I can achieve. My company could have become bigger, ten or twenty or even a hundred times bigger than we are, but I don't take that kind of challenge. I am very happy with what I have achieved.

I still work very hard. I wake up early in the morning. I go to my office at eight o'clock and usually finish about twelve hours later. I enjoy it very much. I don't have a fear of going broke. I know how to handle my cash, but I remember what life was like without it and I don't want to go back to those days.

On entering my forties I became much more confident as a citizen of this world; I became a privileged citizen of Great Britain and a role model for the Bangladeshi community. But before I reached this age I was a fighter. Everywhere I went I used make a stand for my cases like I am the desperate minority immigrant, whether it was in England or the USA, Brussels or Milan. That is the truth and it is the message I want to give to my generation: this is the struggle we have gone through for our children to make their lives comfortable in Britain and Bangladesh and anywhere else in the world! I am no expert, but everybody in my generation will say the same thing because we had to fight for our lives against racism. That fight was to prove that I can be just as successful a man as anybody else.

People ask if there is a secret to my success. The idea is the most important thing. You have to have a dream. You have to have the vision. Once you have the vision you have to have the drive and the energy to follow it through. The vision for me started when I saw my father in his shop in Oldham. I could see it was a business that my family needed, but at the same time I knew I did not want to stand behind the counter. After a while I realised that wholesale, not retail, was the future for me. Then it was just a matter of hard work.

Coming to England was another vision. I was always encouraging my family. I kept saying, 'Let's go!' I knew it was the right thing to do. If I had said to my grandmother, 'I don't want to go to England. I want to stay here. I have lots of friends that I don't want to leave. I don't want to go abroad,' things would have been different, but I said, 'No. Let us go to England.' And they listened to me because I am the oldest son.

Ambition is very important but it is also very, very important who you associate with. You have to be very selective in choosing your friends. I have made a lot of friends and associates over the years. I found that some friends can be greedy for power. They can be ruthless at times and might l put you down in pursuit of their own ambitions. It is sometimes difficult to judge a person. You have to follow your instinct. You want friends who will be there for you and with you along the way. Friends that you can count on to help you fulfil your ambition.

I knew the wholesale business would be successful very quickly, as soon as I started to buy and sell and see the profit to be made. When we were running the shop and deliveries of products arrived in a big truck, I immediately realised those companies delivering were in a better business than we were. There they were, with one driver and one helper, picking up goods from London, delivering to us, taking the money and then leaving. There we were trying to serve hundreds of people; sometimes the goods were not of good quality and sometimes we gave credit that we didn't get paid for, and we had at the same time all the huge responsibilities of running the shop. I could see straight away that the wholesale people had a better business with much more potential than simply selling. I thought about it more and decided I wanted to become a manufacturer.

That was another early wise decision. I saw the potential of manufacture. One step leads to another. You have the vision, and you plan as you go along, and it's very important you find the right people to advise you along the way. I was pleased by my progress but it was never enough. There are always new areas to explore, new challenges to take on. It is not so much that I am never satisfied; it is that I am always building and growing my business.

Life is all about making the right decisions, and sometimes that means listening to the right advice. My mother was against me becoming an MP. She was right, I realise now. I think I could have been an effective MP. I have the knowledge now and the experience, but I am pleased I did not go into politics. I believe I have achieved much more outside. Also, several years ago, I was offered a nomination for a seat in the House of Lords by a former Bangladesh High Commissioner to the UK. He invited me to his office in London. I was puzzled as to why and asked, 'Your Excellency, thank you for inviting me. Why have you invited me?' He said, 'Iqbal, what I have to say is very important. Sit down and listen to me.' He went on to explain that Bangladesh had only one representative in the House of Lords and he thought that was not good enough.

Other countries like Pakistan and India had far more people and far more influence. 'We would like another person to represent us in the House of Lords,' he said. 'We would like you to be that person!'

I was quite overwhelmed by his suggestion. He wanted to nominate me. I thought about it. In fact I thought very deeply about it and then I said it was too early. This was many years ago, and I did not feel I was ready for such an honour or such a responsibility. I thought about what I had done in my life very carefully. I considered that my children were still young and my business was not yet settled, and I was working so hard, I thought I would struggle if I took this on. All my business would have been destroyed because had I been an adviser to the government, with meetings four or five times a year, it would have taken so much of my time.

So I said, 'Your Excellency, thank you very much for the suggestion but I cannot accept at this time, it is simply too soon. I know that not many people do not receive such an amazing offer, but I think it is too early for me.' He didn't like my answer but he accepted it and in the end said, 'Very well, the decision is yours.' Although I am very grateful to him, I think with hindsight it was the right decision to make. In the future, you never know.

I also had a proposal to become a member of parliament in Bangladesh. It came from the local party committee. I talked to my mother about it and she said, 'In the environment you have grown up in, can you honestly say to your constituents you are local? It will be difficult to communicate with them. It might have a negative impact coming back from England to be an MP in Bangladesh.'

She then advised, 'Do not say no.' I was puzzled: 'So what

215

do I do?' I think at one stage I wanted to tell the press, 'Look I am just not interested. I don't want to become an MP.' She said, 'Don't do that. Just say you are not ready yet. If you give a flat refusal you might upset the government. They can see you have potential even though you don't want to do it.' She told me to say that when I was ready I would let them know, otherwise they might think I was supporting the opposition. That was more diplomatic and she was absolutely right of course, as mothers so often are. It was very good advice.

CHAPTER THIRTY

SAD LOSSES

MY GRANDMOTHER

My paternal grandfather died on 17 December 1972 and after he passed away, my grandmother continued to live in Bangladesh. She came to England in 1987 and stayed with us for quite some time, but her home was where her heart lay. She went back to Bangladesh and enjoyed the rest of her life in the place she loved. She was very well looked after by my mother and some of our close relatives and friends. She died peacefully at home on 10 October 2001. Salma, my wife, and I were by her side during her last hours. Losing my grandmother was one of the saddest moments of my life.

MY FATHER

My father became quite ill later in his life. I can remember the day he died. I was flying to Bangladesh that day, and he was in the UK at the time. He was in hospital for observation, so I went to visit him and to ask for his blessings. Although he looked tired, he was smiling and in good spirits. We had a good chat and I left feeling happy. As soon as I landed in Dubai for my connecting flight to Bangladesh I heard that my father had passed away. I cannot explain the shock of hearing this most tragic news. I could not believe it. We had had a good talk that morning and he had seemed fine. I would not have left him otherwise. I flew back home as soon as I could get a ticket. All I could think of was my mother and my siblings and the pain we were all going through. As the new head of the family I had to be strong for everybody.

MY MOTHER

All my life I called my mother Amma. She was my best teacher. Like my grandmother, she was a source of inspiration. I learned so much about the values of life from my mother. She was a perfectionist. She never compromised in her life. She was hard to please: there were many occasions where I had to exchange something that I bought her because she did not like it. Her choice always came first, something we all learned to accept, including my father. She knew what she wanted and she would tell you so. She was frank, but never rude.

My mother was not very educated. Everything she learned was from her experiences in life. When I was in high school, I can remember that the telephone was almost non-existent where we lived, so at weekends she made it my job to write her letters to family and friends. Between us we also used to do our budgeting in the evening. I know now that encouraging me to do all those exercises was her way of helping to develop my knowledge.

I never stopped being a child whenever Amma, my mother,

was around. Even as I grew older, and until she died, I was her little boy. In my mid-forties, I spent a lot of time with Amma in Bangladesh whilst expanding my business there. I made a lot of new friends during that time, and I used to go out with them and travel to places further away. One night I did not come home until well past midnight. It was almost 2.30 a.m. I slowly walked through the garden leading to our house. When I reached the main door, I heard Amma call, 'Is that Iqbal?' It was dark and she was sitting in her rocking chair. She startled me; I was also shocked that she'd waited for me all this time as she normally retired for bed early. She said she was worried that something had happened to me. I felt so bad and made sure from then on I would let her know if I was going to be late.

Amma loved Bangladesh and she loved living there. Like my father, she looked after people around us. She helped them financially. She enjoyed feeding them, talking to them, and buying them clothes, especially during religious occasions. She loved celebrating with them. She was a very generous woman. Amma came back to the UK to live with me before she passed away on 5 August 2012. One day she asked me if she could return to Bangladesh, so I asked my sister, Rahela to go with her. My mother was not very well at the time so Salma and I took her to see her doctor before she left.

She fell very ill within two weeks of arriving in Bangladesh. She had problems breathing. Dr Dev, our family doctor called to tell me that my Amma was very ill and I must come soon. He eventually told me that Amma might have cancer. It was a big blow. Kamal, my brother, and I went immediately. Amma never liked hospital so she was at home and a nurse was with her. She was on oxygen to help with her breathing. There was bleeding from her lungs. We did not waste time. I called my friend, Tapan Chowdhury, straight away. He is the managing director of Square Hospital and he requested an ambulance. He sent an air ambulance and I went in the helicopter with Amma. We were told at the hospital that her condition was very serious and could not be treated there and the nearest hospital where she could be treated was in Singapore.

It took four hours by air ambulance to get to Singapore. Kamal and his wife were with Amma. I took a separate flight and met them there. She had all the tests necessary and was very well looked after by doctors and staff. Amma was in Singapore for a month; myself, Kamal and his wife Sulthana and daughter Fahmin all took turns to be with Amma. She was always with one of us and was never left on her own. After a month, the oncologist suggested that we should take her to The Christie hospital in Manchester, England. So we went back to Dhaka and then to Manchester. Amma lived for another nine months. She regularly went for hospital visits and appointments. This became a normality for us all. Salma and Bilal's wife, Komol, took great care of her and were with Amma all the time.

She passed away peacefully in our house during the month of Ramadan in 2012, surrounded by her family and everyone that she loved, and those who loved her in return.

I miss Amma every day.

CHAPTER THIRTY-ONE

MY TEAM

I always believe in hard work. I know I have said so quite a few times. People often tell me when they meet me, 'Oh you are extremely lucky!' Sometimes they put me down, but this is how some people communicate. I imagine that considering where I come from and what I have done in the Western world, they believe they have the right to say anything. I believe in hard work and I believe in preparation. Plus you have to be lucky nowadays because there is so much competition around. But without hard work, preparation and making the right decisions at the right time you can't be lucky. So I am lucky.

The most important thing is who is with you. I have genuinely been extremely lucky to be surrounded by some wonderful people. So many nice people just came to be part of my journey.

My family, of course, are part of that. I am lucky to have a beautiful and intelligent wife, great children and grandchildren. My wife is a great lady. She has helped me the whole way in everything I wanted to do. And, of course, my two brothers. I would not have become successful without them by my side.

And there are people in my workplace who have been so supportive also. There are so many of them, I can only name a few. My first office manager was Jim Carpenter. He started in the early eighties and he worked until right up to the last day of his retirement. He worked hard and he was really dedicated; he looked after everything in the office. One thing about Jim was that he always wanted to see me in the Queen's Honours List because he saw my social work activities, the work I do for communities, promotion of Bangladeshi products and my contribution to export. Jim always thought that I should get an honour. He used to tell me a story about his brother, who was a canon somewhere in Ireland. 'You are making more contributions than my brother,' he said. 'He has got an MBE, you will have an OBE one day. I would like to see it.' But unfortunately we lost touch before I received the OBE. Jim Carpenter made a huge contribution to my company in the early days.

Then there was John Healey, who was my import manager. It is quite an important post in my company because what we import has to be well planned, well negotiated, and it needs to be ensured that the cost is right. His office was always close to mine and he made a huge contribution to the company. Unfortunately, he became ill after his retirement and very sadly passed away not long afterwards.

I want to mention somebody else, Sue Stockley, a remarkable lady. She started working on reception and moved on from there to various jobs within our company. She was in payroll and HR and then she became an office manager. Sue was a very popular lady, everybody liked her. She always worked hard for the company. If she saw things wrong she would put them right; she used to correct me sometimes as well! She was like a big sister in our company and in our family. She was always there to help. When my elder daughter got married she helped organise everything. Sadly, Sue had to leave the company for health reasons. She died of cancer in 2014.

There are many people still with me to mention. Yasmin Nimakwala, who joined as a young woman, has been faithfully working for me for twenty-five years. She is so reliable I must thank her for her wonderful service. Yasmin is very proud to work for Seamark and she has her own thoughts: 'I love working for Mr Iqbal. He is a great boss who is very fair with everyone. He can be firm but he is also very kind. Sometimes when an employee is ill or suffering from a problem he has quietly helped them out or paid for treatment. He is a good man. I am proud to work for him.'

I would also like to mention another valued member of staff, Barry Minnery, a latecomer who was Alec's replacement. Barry has helped me a lot since his appointment in early 2010. He has been very supportive and I rely on him for advice on many different matters. 'I first met Iqbal Ahmed late in 2009 when Seamark was looking to recruit a successor to the previous Financial Controller who had retired some years earlier without being directly replaced. Iqbal was looking for someone not only with the skills and expertise to guide an already very successful business through the new challenges presented by the far reaching consequences of the financial crisis but who also had the personality to fit into the culture of the family owned business.

'For some reason known only to him he gave me the job and over the next four years we worked closely to reshape and restructure the business to ensure its continued success before I handed over the full time reins at the end of 2013 and accepted Iqbal's invitation to take up a part time advisory and strategic role.

'I have therefore been fortunate to experience at first hand Iqbal's hugely impressive qualities: the scope of his vision as to how the business can develop and grow; the ability to identify those niche areas of the markets which his businesses can exploit; the confidence and courage to back his judgement with investment even in challenging times; the drive to get the job done overcoming barriers and obstacles; the ability to inspire others to high levels of achievement and fulfil potential and the commitment and dedication to providing the highest standards of customer service.

'Iqbal's leadership qualities and standing are never better on show than at the annual Seafood Expo Global Exhibition in Brussels where he is equally at home representing and promoting the company in dealings with diplomats, politicians and businessmen; entertaining customers; identifying opportunities and supporting sales staff in pursuing orders and enquiries.

'Iqbal's high and respected profile within the Bangladesh expatriate community has enabled him to make a positive and significant contribution to the development of bilateral trade between the UK and Bangladesh and I know he takes particular pride in two achievements in this respect.

'As a founder and first Chairman of NRB Bank he was able to secure the backing, expertise and funding to meet the capital and regulatory requirements for a new bank operating in Bangladesh providing new banking services.

'As founder and Chairman of UK Bangladesh Catalysts of Commerce and Industry (UKBCCI) he was successful in securing support within the Bangladesh community to establish a body to promote trade and development between Bangladesh and UK.

'Through his detailed knowledge of the global seafood industry he has become a true revolutionary introducing new products into Europe and opening up new supply routes in the developing world.

'He has been supportive professionally and personally and I have the highest regard for his remarkable business achievements; entrepreneurial spirit, integrity and humanity and feel honoured and privileged to have him as a boss, business colleague and personal friend.'

The latest addition to my senior members of staff is Nigel Fowles, my current Financial Controller who took over from Barry. He's been with me for over three years and is doing a very good job. He is reliable and I can count on him.

There are so many good people working with us and without their support it would be impossible to run an empire like ours, which now has over 4,000 people working with us. I have to mention the gentleman who is my father's first cousin, Mr Tohurul Islam. He was a professor who studied in England and went to Japan to do his PhD and various jobs. I finally pulled him back to my company. He is an executive director and another highly respected person in the organisation.

I have Shamsul Islam Khan who is our general manager and another dedicated person in my life who has put in so much effort towards our success. Our chief engineer is Salil Mitra, another dependable person who has also been with me for a few decades. Part of the reason I sleep easily is that my team is so hard-working and faithful. I can rely on every one of them. One of my cousins, Shanoor, has also been with us for many years. He has been with me from his childhood, taking care of me, and our organisation, with total dedication.

The most important lady in my life, after my immediate family, is Nita Shah, my executive assistant. She has been with me since soon after she came to this country. She is married to a handsome engineer and I remember when she started in our company. He used to pick her up every day! She was a very silent, very quiet young lady. Over the years Nita has become so important that everybody relies on her. I certainly do. I value her opinion and her contribution to the company. She manages and controls many things for me and the business. Nita has become invaluable to me, as she has been for many years, and it would be very difficult for me to replace her.

Nita Shah says: 'It has been a privilege to see how the company has grown from just Jim Carpenter and me in the office to thousands of employees worldwide. It has meant a great deal to me to witness that growth and be a part of it.

'When I came to England I lived in London for nearly a year before moving to Manchester. I have worked for Mr Iqbal since the summer of 1989. We were in a small office when I joined; there was just me and Jim Carpenter in one room and Mr Iqbal and Mr Kamal in another. Bilal joined later.

'My job title was: Sales Invoice Clerk. It was the era of the telex machine and Mr Iqbal taught me how to operate it. I had not seen one before never mind used it. It was Iqbal Bros & Company then, and there were only a few men in the cold store, a couple of drivers and the three brothers. Back then, I often used to see Mr Iqbal drive the forklift truck and help in the loading and unloading of containers. Mr Kamal and Bilal did the same. They worked very hard, for long hours and through most weekends. They were dedicated and determined to succeed. With that dedication and hard work Seamark was made possible.

'I was allowed to work part-time for a few years after the birth of my daughter. When I came back to work full-time Mr Iqbal was looking for a secretary. We did some advertising and I had arranged some interviews for him. I cannot remember what happened, but no one had been appointed. One day he called me into his office and offered me the job as his assistant. It was unexpected. I was quite nervous, worried because I was not sure I was up to it. "You can do it," he said, and that was it. I had varied duties, but assisting Mr Iqbal was my primary role. It still is today, I am happy to say. I am honoured for the opportunity that he has given me to assist him and very grateful to him for trusting me to work alongside him. We have mutual respect for each other and he is a brilliant boss.

'I had been offered another job before I had my interview with Mr Iqbal. I did not know which job to take but this one was nearer for me, just one bus ride away. That was the deal-breaker. But taking this job was the best decision I have ever made. The business has grown into something that I could never have imagined. It is a very competitive business but with Mr Iqbal's leadership, decisiveness and forward thinking Seamark remains ahead. We are lucky to have a leader like him.

'He is always looking for ways to improve, develop and innovate. Mr Iqbal is an inspiration to us all. He sees the good and the potential in people. It is a privilege to work with a genius. He is passionate about the business and he likes getting involved with everything, down to every small detail. He expects his staff to work hard and to respect each other.

He wants people to learn from him and he enjoys learning from other people. I often hear him say, "You learn every day," when something goes wrong. That sometimes happens but he does not let it upset him. He sees it as an opportunity and takes it as something he must learn from. He turns a negative into a positive. Mr Iqbal makes decisions very quickly. He is very loyal especially to those who have remained loyal to him. He also does not forget people that helped him along the way.

'Charity is something he makes time for. He holds fund-raising events to raise money for different charities in the UK and Bangladesh. He also raised funds to help victims of calamities in Bangladesh. He personally gets involved as much as he can. He is very generous, not just with his money but also with his time and his knowledge. He gets invited a lot as a speaker or a panellist to many international and national events. He makes the effort to participate as he wants to share his experiences, knowledge and vision.

'Mr Iqbal's family means the world to him. He loves them greatly and makes time for them no matter how busy he is. They are his priority and they always come first. He loves his wife dearly and he is very proud of his children and what they have achieved. He dotes on his two granddaughters, Parisa and Amira. He fondly talks about them and cannot wait for them to grow up. He is very funny, and has an amazing sense of humour. He used to make Sue Stockley and I laugh so much. You don't get bored when he's around. He is full of life and I admire his energy. He travels all the time. I don't really know how he does it.

'He takes great care of his appearance. He always comes in the office smartly dressed and I have never seen his shoes unpolished. He likes to be different and has his own style. He wears vibrant colours and can carry it off with no problem. Confidence is something he does not lack. He is by no means perfect – no one is, but he does things perfectly and just the way he wants it.

Mr Iqbal is the thinker, the leader and the driving force of the business. With Mr Kamal and Bilal behind him, anything is possible. There is no limit.

The human relationship with my team is very, very important to me. I think it is the key to my success. Without good people like these I would not have achieved so much. My success is their success also. Without professional people like these you can't make your company successful. You can't make your life successful. There are many others, a few hundred perhaps, who have been very helpful too, but these are the key people for the past two or three decades. I simply love them. They are part of my life. I need to talk to them every day.

CHAPTER THIRTY-TWO

CHILDREN

My children are the lights of my life. I am so proud of my two daughters, Shahida and Hamida, and son Manzur. They are all such an important part of everything I do that I must tell you about them here. I have always enjoyed spending time with my children, especially when they were young – we went on so many holidays to different parts of the world. I never missed a parents' evening. I liked to know how they were doing in school and I wanted them to know that I was taking an interest in their education. I want them to feel proud that I have time for them.

Shahida, my older daughter, was brilliant at school. She completed her Bachelor of Medicine and Bachelor of Surgery degree at Leeds University. She also completed a BSc with honours during her medical training. Shahida then undertook General Practitioner training in the North West and London Deaneries. During her GP training she took time out to have two children. She has now completed the Membership of the Royal College of GPs and is currently a GP in Fulham, London. She is married to Mahiul Muhammed Khan Muqit, or Mahi, who is a consultant vitreo-retinal surgeon at Moorfields Eye Hospital in London. Mahi also works with Helen Keller International on several innovative projects in Bangladesh in the field of diabetic eye disease and blindness prevention.

Nowadays, I really enjoy spending time with their daughters, my two granddaughters. They are my little princesses and I adore them. They used to live in Wilmslow, Cheshire, so when they were younger my wife and I were able to spend some very enjoyable times with them. Parisa Maha Muqit is the older of the two. She is eight years old now and attends Putney High School for Girls. She enjoys children's poetry and languages and loves to spend time with her grandparents during the holidays. Her younger sister, Amira Soha Muqit, is five years old and goes to the same school. She enjoys sports, baking with her mummy and also, I'm delighted to say, spending time with her grandparents! I hope they will both be proud of their grandfather when they are older.

Manzur, my only son, is the next oldest after Shahida. Now thirty-four, he is quite an independent character. He was always good at education, working very hard at school and at university. He has travelled all over the world. Manzur focuses very hard on whatever he does and likes to be ahead of everything. He works for the company, in charge of the hospitality division, and he also runs the Vermilion restaurant. He is in charge of all the wedding venue functions. He is building up that side of the business. We are building a hotel and he will be in charge. He is very capable, very smart and I am very proud of him. In September 2015, he got married to

Sarah in Paris, where she was born. They are both very happy. Sarah is a very beautiful young lady and has adapted to our family and our culture. They make a lovely couple. At the moment they are living with us, I am delighted to say. There is plenty of room!

Hamida is a very independent girl. She is very creative and she designs her own dresses and enjoys designing for others too. She dances very well and she is the best choreographer in the family. She can also sing; she is very culturally minded. She joined the company after finishing her master's degree, starting in my HR department, and she is now a director in the company responsible for exporting. She reports to my brother Kamal and both of them concentrate on exports. She works hard and she is very able. Again, she is focused, a team leader who takes her role seriously. I am very lucky to have her. She also takes the lead in designing some of our brochures. Hamida likes to get involved with everything. She is very confident and I know that I can count on her. I think she has a bright future.

It is great to have Manzur and Hamida as well as my nephew Rubayeth and niece Fahmida coming up behind and supporting the business. They all work very hard and get involved in various activities in addition to their main duties. It has grown so much that it is no longer a 'family business', but it is great to have members of the family rising within it. I am proud of all three of my children, very proud.

CHAPTER THIRTY-THREE

THE LANDSEER

We lived in Oldham for many years before we moved to Cheshire. We had a very comfortable house with big beautiful garden and a swimming pool. The house was named Copster House. In the mid-nineties, Salma and I made the decision to move out of Oldham and into Cheshire and became determined to find the family home most suited to us and our three children. We spent a few years searching with no hope and no luck.

For as long as I could remember, I had always wanted to build my own house to match my desires. This dream of mine grew into a passion as time went on. Whilst I was away on a business trip, a house in Cheshire had caught Salma's attention. She felt it had been the house we were looking for and had the potential to become our family home for many years to come. Although I wished to build at the time, I thought the process would be lengthy and complicated and I need to find a piece of land.

Nevertheless, the house my wife had seen had the potential and we began the negotiations. Along the way, many friends tried to discourage us from buying this particular property for various reasons. But we were content and wanted to move in quickly so as not to interfere with the children's schooling.

We lived in this house named Merithorn for thirteen years, refurbishing the entire property over the years. We constructed a pond feature, a conservatory, a bigger garage and tennis court. While out on a walk with Salma one summer's day, we noticed a house for sale nearby. The location was perfect and the house was built on a large piece of land. The house itself looked tired and needed a facelift! But I really liked the land and thought it the perfect place upon which to build my dream home. The following day, I called a friend at the estate agents to make some enquiries and learned that the house was sold and in the final stages of negotiation. I told my friend that we liked the house and asked whether he could find out if the vendor would renegotiate with us and left it at that as I was to go on a business trip the next day. I was in Singapore and remembered calling the estate agent asking for any news. I was so happy when he said that the vendor was willing to negotiate with us. Thankfully, it was successful and few months later, the house was ours.

We used a very well-known architect that had good ties with the local council, and although there were stumbling blocks along the way and refusals from the council, we were finally granted planning permission. The gruelling task of demolishing the existing house and building my dream home began with the help of British architects and builders and French interior designers.

This project took a few years to complete. It has taken a lot of my time and effort as I was involved in every aspect of the building. This meant I was able to fulfil my lifelong desire of building my own house the way I wanted it to be. This house means a lot to me and I wanted it to have a very meaningful name. My son Manzur suggested we name it The Landseer. When my father first moved to England before we came to join him, he bought a house on Landseer Street in Oldham. This was our first family house. It had many memories I hold dear and it was where I spent most of my youth. These memories have never left me and hold the foundations of my life. It is fitting that I called my dream home The Landseer.

In June 2013, my family and I moved into The Landseer.

CHAPTER THIRTY-FOUR

MY THOUGHTS

I want to say a few things from my heart, about how I feel about my life and my experience. I want to explain my feelings about looking after other people and the challenges I took. I always enjoyed taking on challenges, I enjoyed learning and at the same time, I enjoyed inspiring other people, as well as sharing my success.

My family is all-important to me. All of my life I have enjoyed being a member of a large and happy family. I have always been very proud of and determined to respect my parents. They looked after me with great kindness when I was young and I wanted to care for them when I became older. Sadly they are no longer with us. I still think about them a great deal and I never regret a single moment of the life that I enjoyed with them. I hope I never made them upset or concerned because of my behaviour.

Likewise, in the same way I have enjoyed enormously seeing

my children grow up. It has been an enormous privilege and pleasure to watch them develop through the years and to give them the best education possible. I always wanted to make them happy throughout. It gave me the greatest satisfaction. My parents, my brothers and sisters, and my wife, children and grandchildren, and all the members of my family are so important to me. My extended family is large, but I care deeply for them all and I am always trying to take care of them. Taking caring of them and loving them is one of the most enjoyable things I have done. All of the members of my large family are important to me. I like to look after everyone if I can. That is my mission in life! If I can look after my sisters and brothers and feed them well I feel satisfied. These are my most important feelings. I think this is probably one of the reasons I work so hard. I feel driven to do my level best for the family. That is my role.

Since childhood I have been doing social work. For example, if I am going to a city and somebody wants something and says, 'Will you get me this medicine or get me this item,' I will try to buy it for them. I always wanted to make people, family and friends, happy. It does not matter who they are or where they are from. I deal with many different nationalities.

I love people and it gives me great pleasure to love and to be loved in return. I appreciate the affection. I know that sometimes when people want me to be involved in their company and to spend time with me, they wait for months. People have parties and invite me and I appreciate that very much. I suppose I am larger than life. I am fortunate that I have the energy and the ability to do well and I want to share my good fortune with everyone I know.

I have taken on some big challenges and fortunately I have

been successful in most of them. I believe life is for living and living to the full. I want to help people and of course, I must be frank, at the same time I have also enjoyed making money, I have found it creative to work hard and fulfil my ambitions. Spending money also gives me great satisfaction. I have spent well, I have travelled well; I have bought and built beautiful houses, and had the best cars. I love to wear the best clothes, and I have provided the same for my children and my wife and other members of my family. We all enjoy it.

There are many people I know who enjoy making money but they can't spend it. They don't know how to spend or they have no time to spend. I am very comfortable with myself; I have had hard times and difficult moments in my life, and people always think that I am relaxed, that I take it all so easily, but deep down I feel it from the heart.

During every stage of my life, I always believe I have done enough. Maybe tomorrow I'll go and buy an island. That's something different, but in fact I think I have achieved enough. To buy an island and become lord of that island would be like something from a dream or in miracle. It could happen, but whatever I have achieved up to this moment I am happy enough with. I am more than comfortable with my life. I didn't copy anything or anyone. Everything I did came from my own heart and my own head.

We come into this world with nothing and we will leave this world with nothing. I hope people will remember me not because of my wealth but for the good things I have done; I want them to be my legacy. Money is not everything. It makes your life more comfortable and it is great to be able to make the lives of your nearest and dearest more comfortable, too. But it is not everything. As long as you are truly happy in your mind and in your heart that is more important than anything else in the world. This is what I truly believe, that money and wealth is not everything. Happiness comes much more from doing good deeds and caring for your family.

Regarding the business, I know some people who are afraid of competition, but competition is everywhere as soon as you step out of your door in the morning. You can come out of your house and see your neighbour has a better car than you and discover that his children are getting a better education than yours; when you go to work you can discover someone else is producing a new product that is better than yours. It is no good getting upset in such situations. I have never been afraid of competition. Other people's successes have never made me feel uncomfortable. I have never been a jealous person. I believe there is room in life for other people to achieve success as well as myself. There will always be other more successful people who make more money than me. That is OK.

I know some people are smarter and cleverer and more successful than me and that is fine, too. It doesn't make me feel jealous, which is important. I can appreciate the success of other people. I am God gifted because I don't come across those kinds of people. I like sharing my success and I like to share the secret of my success. I give people good advice and I want to see them become successful. I enjoy it very much when they do. I don't like to boast that I made a lot of people successful, but over the years I have given a lot of good advice, and a lot of people have become successful from nothing. I know people from thirty or forty years ago, or even as far back as my childhood days, to whom I have given advice and often helped to find opportunities. Many of them have become successful. These are the people I love and it makes me so happy to see them doing well.

I have written much about the importance of my family and my friends to me, their help and support and encouragement, the joy of seeing them and being among them. But I could not have come this far without other friends with whom, for whatever reason, it has proved impossible to stay or remain in touch. Each and every one of them has been a part of my journey through life, and absence or distance or other obstacles do not mean that they are not always in my heart.

Nothing is impossible in life. You can make things that seem impossible possible if you work hard; with dedication and hard work anything is achievable. Create your own vision and never be afraid to go for a challenge. That is what I have found. I believe that deeply. My life is full of success and there is no room in it for regrets. I have no regrets. I don't mind taking on more challenges in the future – and I am sure they will come my way.